45 Trips on the Northwest's Inland Waters

KAYAKING

Puget Sound,
the San Juans,
and Gulf Islands

---

by Randel Washburne

THE MOUNTAINEERS

The Mountaineers: Organized 1906 ". . . *to explore, study, preserve, and enjoy the* *natural beauty of the Northwest.*"

© 1990 by Randel Washburne

4   3   2
5   4   3   2

Published by The Mountaineers
1011 S.W. Klickitat Way, Suite 107, Seattle, Washington 98134

Published simultaneously in Canada by Douglas & McIntyre, Ltd.,
1615 Venables Street, Vancouver, B.C. V5L 2H1

Published simultaneously in Great Britain by Cordee
3a DeMontfort St., Leicester, England LE1 7HD

Manufactured in the United States of America

Edited by Miriam Bulmer
Maps by Helen Sherman
Cover photograph by David Harrison
All other photographs by the author
Cover design by Constance Bollen
Book design and layout by Bridget Culligan

Library of Congress Cataloging in Publication Data
Washburne, Randel.
   Kayaking Puget Sound, the San Juans and Gulf Islands : 45 trips
on the Northwest's inland waters / by Randel Washburne.
      p.   cm.
   Includes bibliographical references.
   ISBN 0-89886-189-6
   1. Sea kayaking--Northwest, Pacific--Guide-books. 2. Northwest,
Pacific--Description and travel--Guide-books.   I. Title.
GV788.5.W39 1990
797.1'22'0979--dc 20   89-78381
                                                              CIP

Acknowledgments

To those who contributed their expertise: Dr. David Burch (Star-path School of Navigation), Dr. Harold Mofjeld (NOAA), Dave Castor, Will Lorentz, Doug Peznecker, Tom Snyder (all Washington State Parks), John Garrett (Washington Department of Wildlife), Judy Friesem (Washington Department of Ecology), Dave Duggins (Nature Conservancy), Rick Kiesser (Washington State Ferries), and Ellie Henke (U.S. Fish and Wildlife Service).

To those willing to share their local knowledge: Tom Carter, Tim Davis, Oscar Lind, Chris Mork, Judy and Lee Moyer (Lee's efforts to improve paddling opportunities along the Duwamish Waterway are a service to us all), Tom Myers, Stan Reeve, Neville Richter, Bill Ross, Marion Slater, Tom Steinburn, Kelly Tjaden, and Bill Turner.

To those who assisted me in my explorations: Kevin Cron, Linda Daniel, Mike and Susan Huffman, Dwight Jacobson, Keith Maclean, Mitch Press, Hank Snelgrove, Bill Turner, and Mom.

To those who helped me make this book: Margaret Foster-Finan, Steve Whitney, Miriam Bulmer, Marge Mueller, and (for her advice on the first edition and on my becoming a book writer in the first place) Linda Daniel.

And to my wife Gunvor, for her patience and support.

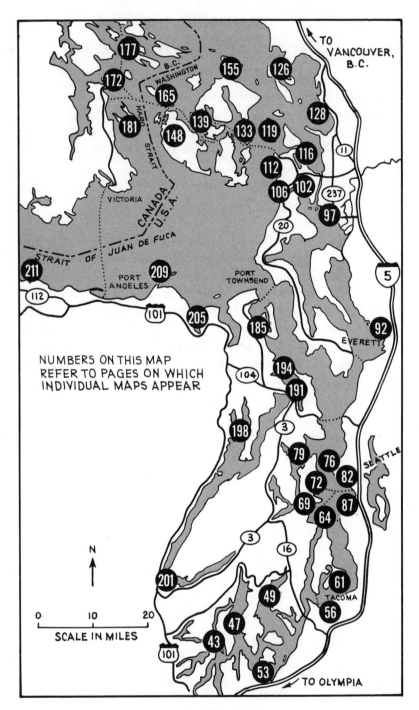

NUMBERS ON THIS MAP
REFER TO PAGES ON WHICH
INDIVIDUAL MAPS APPEAR

N

0   10   20
SCALE IN MILES

Table of Contents

Introduction

The Pacific Northwest has a national reputation as prime boating country, and its extensive inland waterways are considered among the best in the world for sea kayaking. The attributes that make good boating of any kind also make good paddling—beautiful scenery, intricate and protected waterways, clear and clean water, abundant marine life, and a lot more. On shore there are ample public parklands, many on islands where the original wild charm still is strong.

The kayaker's perspective on his or her surroundings is a bit different from that of other boaters. And from the close-to-the-water and close-to-the-land perspective, the Pacific Northwest reveals an extra, appealing dimension.

For self-propelled boaters, shoreline is everything. It is along the shoreline that most of us prefer to direct our travels, rather than heading out across open water. We experience it at touching distance within the intertidal zone: holding to a rock while drifting by on a calm afternoon; leaning back to look straight up at the brick red trunk of a madrona against the blue sky; lingering beneath the city's piers on a quiet Sunday morning to watch the sun illuminate the anemone-coated pilings below.

Shorelines here have "texture," a word that expresses all the things that make it interesting: the spongelike eroded sandstones of Sucia Island; the crumbling canneries along Guemes Channel; the tiny channels that, at high tide, meander inland for miles through the Nisqually Flats' marshlands. Few other boaters know this texture as kayakers do. In these places we meet the creatures that other boaters scarcely see at all: myriad sea- and shorebirds, river otters, and orcas. Kayakers share a special relationship with their most common traveling companion, the shy but curious harbor seal, and experience humorous aspects such as the seal's embarrassment when you make eye contact with him.

Just as kayakers look to the land for enjoyment, we also look to the sea—and we like how it treats us in the Pacific Northwest. Sea kayakers from the stormy, unsheltered British Isles coast comment that paddling is so *easy* here. With our winding inland channels and frequently docile winds, that is a valid observation. At least during the warmer months, sunny highs drift in to stay for weeks, breezes are languid, and kayakers overtake sailors too stubborn to motor.

Particularly in the San Juan and Gulf islands' powerful tide races, kayaks can pass the sailboats with hardly a stroke, threading behind the kelp beds in back eddies along the shores. Our currents are at once a threat and a blessing, contributing significantly to the Northwest's paddling identity with their free rides and perilous tide rips. Probably more than for any other kind of boater, the kayaker is engaged by both the positive and negative aspects of moving salt water. In the Northwest, we quickly learn the currents' workings, for an opposing current can make rough seas murderous. In these waters, the whitewater paddler can find something reminiscent of the river drops back home, while the more contemplative sightseer can regard currents through streaming, swaying kelp beds on long downstream runs.

In short, saltwater kayaking hardly needs selling to Pacific Northwesterners. Thousands have already discovered its charms, and sea kayaks are becoming a significant craft among the pleasure vessels cruising the waterways. New kayakers come to it from diverse backgrounds. Many aficionados of self-propelled terrestrial travel—backpackers, cross-country skiers—have found in kayaks an agreeable and reasonably priced way to explore a whole new realm. Marine channels open up to them like an unexplored network of trails. For whitewater river paddlers, many skills transfer easily.

Even experienced saltwater boaters have discovered the comparative simplicity of kayak travel and its special relationship to the surroundings. An ex-sailor recalls his dissatisfaction with experiences under sail—boredom liberally laced with exasperation at our typically fluky winds. His experiences with paddle in hand are uniformly more interesting, less sedentary, and less stressful. Other converts speak of the new level of intimacy with the seashore that kayaking brings.

"In the San Juans, there were so many places I'd passed countless times, but never *seen,* being too busy worrying about staying off enough to avoid scraping my keel. And it was just too much trouble to anchor and go ashore. It's like I have a whole new place to explore!"

Others revel in trading the cramped accommodations on board for spacious campsites on shore, gladly swapping 16 hours of motoring from Seattle to the San Juan Islands (after waiting in line at the Hiram Chittenden Locks) for two hours on the highway, perhaps followed by a ferry ride. And not least, monthly loan and moorage payments for a large boat cannot compare to a one-time, $1,000 investment in a kayak, which stores free of charge behind or in the garage.

More than a few sailors and powerboaters in Washington and British Columbia's inland waters have found kayaks to be excellent shore boats—either stowed on decks of larger yachts or towed behind smaller ones. These boaters enjoy the best of both worlds—a quiet evening of solitary paddling along shore plays conterpoint to the challenges or sedentariness of a day under sail or power. Kayaks do have limitations as shore boats. They are poorly suited for carrying bulky gear such as ice chests; can take only as many adults as there are cockpits; and are tricky to get in and out of from boats without a boarding step on the transom.

Kayaks can be towed successfully by sailboats (not faster power-boats) in varying weather conditions. (Though some admit not wanting that additional concern if things get nasty.) Most kayaks track well under tow (one sailor said his kayak needed its nonsteerable skeg down to do so) and are best kept empty and as light as possible. A kayak should have a tightly fitting cockpit cover that will stay on if the kayak should flip. One sailor brings his kayak's bow right up onto his transom in difficult following seas; he says it rides well there. Two kayaks can be towed side by side, with short poles connecting bows and sterns to keep the boats apart and in line with each other.

But this book is not about sea kayaking in general. The focus is confined to saltwater paddling as it relates to this particular region. Despite the focus, this book is not intended to compete with the several fine guidebooks for water goers in this area (listed under Useful Publications). All of the history and much of the shore-based descriptions are too well documented to merit repeating. General boating guides, however, often lack specific information for sea kayakers, information that other boaters find unnecessary and perhaps even peculiar. A few of the guides include a good dose of each local sea's personality. I, too, have tried to add those aspects that are especially attractive or repulsive to kayakers. I also include great many things of interest to kayak visitors on shore that I have not found referenced anywhere else: which beaches are prone to freighters' surge; which campgrounds are usually full (sometimes with other kayakers); which way you should turn to launch your kayak as you stroll off the ferry at Friday Harbor or Winslow; which shore has the eddy that can get you from here to there.

The trips described here are by no means all of the suitable places to have superior sea-kayaking experiences along Pacific Northwest inland waterways, but they are among the best. I used the same criteria in selecting them as in deciding where to dip my own paddle. I focused on loop-trip possibilities so that you can experience new shorelines all the way, though some out-and-back trips are included for their own merits. Wild scenery is always desirable, but I also chose places where development is dominant, yet attractive for its antiquity, interesting for its marine/industrial culture or for the intricacy that over-the-water construction can sometimes present, or perhaps just as a contrast to some tiny pristine enclave. And, since most kayakers are also campers, opportunities for two- or three-day cruises with overnight stopovers are heavily represented along with day trips.

Finally, with some trepidation, I rated saltwater kayak routes in this book by the degree of hazard potential. Much needed, this was as slippery a task as getting a footing on a kelp-covered rock.

All routes are rated as either *Exposed, Moderate,* or *Protected,* ratings which comprise the numerous discrete and sometimes ethereal elements that are the sea environment. Unlike easily rated rivers with predictable conditions that are related to a particular rate of flow, sea conditions change by the minute as winds and currents change in intensity independent of one another. My ratings are based on *potentials* for trouble that may express themselves only rarely, but with perhaps dire consequences: tide rips that spring up from nowhere when the tide changes or a sudden wind that delivers difficult sea conditions during a crossing. There is a real danger that new sea kayakers, lulled by a placid first trip, might be drawn into traps laid by changing weather or tides with few escape routes. I am particularly concerned about weekend trips, where the demands to be home by Sunday night and the lack of a long but easy alternative route leads to "going for it" on a nasty crossing. Sucia Island and its neighboring islands are frequented by weekend neophyte kayakers (my very first overnight paddle was there), yet my criteria led me to rate this trip *Exposed.* (A kayaking fatality did occur in the vicinity in 1985.) My ratings suggest the potential for trouble, based on circumstances and what I and others have encountered there. How you use them depends on your abilities and willingness to take chances.

You might evaluate your own ability to counter the potential sea forces according to your *awareness, strength,* and *survival skills* on the water. Awareness is your ability to anticipate and avoid hazards, for example, to spot a dangerous tide rip far downstream and assess which way to paddle to avoid it. Strength is your ability to paddle hard against wind or current to escape a bad situation. Survival skills on the water are your boat-handling reflexes (balance, braces, or rolls), which enable you to keep going in spite of the sea's energies around you (with the hope that conditions will eventually moderate or that you will reach calmer water).

In my travels around these sounds and islands, the vast majority of times have been good ones. The dangers stay well in the backgound of my recollections without coloring the pleasures. I hope this book can help turn your kayak explorations of these waters into equally fond memories.

A Note on Safety

Sea kayaking entails unavoidable risks that every paddler assumes and must be aware of and respect. The fact that an area or route is described in this book is not a representation that it will be safe for you. Trips vary greatly in difficulty and in the amount and kind of preparation needed to enjoy them safely. On the open ocean and even within the confines of Puget Sound and adjacent waters, conditions can change from day to day, even from hour to hour, owing to weather, currents, tides, shipping activity, and other factors. A trip that is safe in good weather or for a highly conditioned, properly equipped kayaker may be completely unsafe for someone else or unsafe under adverse weather conditions.

You can minimize your risks by being knowledgeable, prepared and alert. There is not space in this book for a general treatise on sea-kayaking technique and safety, but there are good books and public courses on these topics, and you should take advantage of them to increase your knowledge. Do not attempt even the easier routes described in this guidebook unless you have developed basic boat-handling and seamanship skills.

Finally, always be aware of your own limitations and of existing conditions when and where you are traveling. If conditions are dangerous or if you are not prepared to deal with them safely, change your plans! It is better to waste a few hours or perhaps even abandon a long-planned-for trip entirely, than to proceed in the face of dangerous conditions and pay a high price for your insistence.

These warnings are not intended to keep you off the water. Many people enjoy safe sea-kayaking trips in Northwest waters every year. Just remember that one element of the beauty, freedom, and excitement of sea kayaking is the presence of risks that do not confront you at home. When you go sea kayaking, you assume those risks. They can be met safely, but only if you exercise your own independent judgment and common sense.

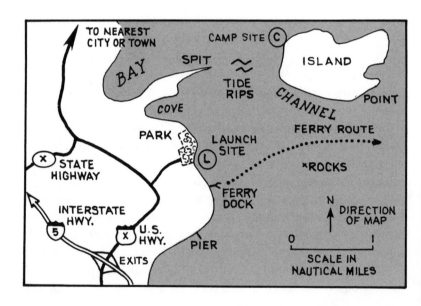

The Pacific Northwest Paddling Environment

Weather, Water, and Marine Shipping

The sea-kayaking environment is always characterized by unpredictable elements, the weather being a primary offender. Northwest marine weather patterns do have some consistencies, and paying attention to both visible signs and marine forecasts can reduce uncertainties and risk about what the weather has in store for you. Another hazard meriting space in this chapter is the chance of being run down by a ship, especially while crossing main traffic channels. As with weather, knowledge about marine traffic can reduce the chances of having a problem. Sea water temperature also deserves cautionary attention. In these waters, immersion and the possibility of hypothermia are a problem serious enough to merit special discussion.

MARINE WEATHER

For kayakers, the most important variable is wind and the resulting sea state. Unfortunately, winds are difficult for meteorologists to forecast, especially in the Pacific Northwest. Visual cues that you can use to predict what is coming are even less reliable, though there are a few I will take note of in this very brief treatment of our local marine weather. For a more thorough understanding of patterns, I recommend Kenneth Lilly's book *Marine Weather of Western Washington* (listed under Useful Publications).

The maritime Northwest's year is almost equally divided into two seasonal weather regimes, each with characteristic patterns. The two regimes are governed by two large atmospheric pressure cells. The Pacific High is always present off the California coast, but expands north in the spring to dominate the entire northeast Pacific until early fall. Then the high retreats south and is replaced by the growing Aleutian Low, which moves south in the fall from the Bering Sea to the Gulf of Alaska and stays through the winter. In spring the low weakens and retreats to the northwest Pacific and the Bering Sea, again replaced with the high.

The summer pattern usually eases in during April and gives way in September. Gales (winds stronger than 33 knots) decrease in frequency toward midsummer as the region becomes dominated by the stable Pa-

Going ashore on Jones Island in the San Juans

cific High pressure, which blocks most disturbances from entering the area. Nonetheless, lows and fronts can bring rain and strong winds, which almost always blow from a southerly direction during bad weather.

During fair weather, winds can still be quite fresh. As the interior landmass warms, air from high-pressure areas in the Pacific Ocean is drawn in through the Strait of Juan de Fuca, where it can blow 25 knots or more in the afternoon. These winds spread to the north and south at the eastern end of the straits, sending southwesterlies up into the San Juan Islands and northwesterlies down across Port Townsend and into northern Puget Sound. Other than as influenced by the Strait of Juan de Fuca, winds tend to be northwesterly during fair weather in the summer regime.

Of course, topography plays an important part in wind direction and force throughout the area. Heating of land creates local onshore winds (called sea breezes) on most sunny afternoons. Hence morning is generally the least windy time for paddling. When the sea breeze direction coincides with the prevailing northwesterly, local winds are intensified.

Mountainous seasides—such as those of Orcas Island—channel winds, deflecting them as much as 90 degrees, and may cause intensified winds where they are forced through a narrow passage or over a saddle between higher hills. For instance, Orcas Island's East Sound often has stronger-than-average winds during prevailing northerlies.

Fog is most common in late July through September, particularly during clear weather when rapid land cooling occurs during the nights. This fog usually clears by early afternoon.

As the Pacific High yields to the Aleutian Low in early fall, prevailing winds shift to southeasterly, and disturbances with gale-force winds become increasingly frequent and intense. The first gales of the season usually occur in late September. By late fall, no weather pattern can be counted on for very long as a procession of unstable fronts and depressions become the rule through the winter. Strong winds are typically southerly throughout the area, but can blow from almost any direction. One particular wintertime hazard is strong northerly winds on clear days, a result of outbreaks from arctic high-pressure fronts located in the interiors of Washington or British Columbia. On the other hand, periods of very calm weather also occur during the winter regime, particularly since the low-angle sun has less power to generate local sea breezes. Fog is also possible, especially in January and February, and may persist for several days.

In keeping an eye out for impending weather, there are a few indicators that suggest changes for the worse. Remember that strong winds can develop from very localized circumstances. Trouble is not necessarily the result of a bad weather system.

In general, be most leery of southerly winds, as these suggest the presence of unsettled weather with potential for strong winds. Oncoming winds often can be spotted on the sea in the distance. Rapid shifts in wind direction, particulary counterclockwise changes ("backing" winds, in nautical parlance) to the southeast suggest the arrival of a front. Whatever the wind direction, weather usually arrives from the west, so note the sky in that direction. The development of high clouds or rings around either the sun or moon are harbingers of a front.

By far the most effective predictor is the meteorologist's marine forecast via VHF radio. Continuous-broadcast forecasts and local weather reports are available from four stations, of which at least one can be tuned in anywhere on Northwest inland waters. In the south sound, NOAA's Olympia station broadcasts on WX3 (162.475 MHz) and NOAA's Seattle station broadcasts on WX1 (162.55 MHz). Canadian stations broadcast similar information on WX2 (162.40 MHz) from Victoria or on WX4 (also called Channel 21B, 161.65 MHz) from

Vancouver. Most "weather radios" or hand-held VHF transceivers get at least the first three of these channels. Forecasts are reissued every six hours, with local-condition updates every three hours.

COLD WATER

Sea temperatures near Seattle vary between 56 degrees (Fahrenheit) in August and 46 degrees in February. Being capsized results in hypothermia—body heat loss that can cause death—unless prompt action is taken to get out of the water. Survival time in 50-degree water can be as little as an hour if you are exerting yourself by swimming (especially when immersing your head), or as much as four hours if you have flotation and are able to hold a heat-retaining fetal position to protect the groin and side areas. Clothing provides some in-the-water insulation (particularly tight weaves and cuffs that trap "dead-water" spaces inside, such as a paddle jacket or semi-dry suit over other garments). Wet or dry suits can extend survival time indefinitely, but most paddlers in this region find them too hot and uncomfortable to wear except in cold weather or times of higher risk.

Hence, well-practiced recovery techniques are especially important in Pacific Northwest waters. Getting out of the water quickly—either back in the boat or ashore—is critical, though hypothermia may continue due to wind chill.

Early stages of hypothermia include violent shivering, but the individual is lucid and talking clearly and sensibly. Short of a warm shower or bath, dry clothes and a chance to sit quietly and warm up (either in a warm place or wrapped up to prevent heat loss) are probably the best treatment.

If shivering is *not* present and/or the person's actions become clumsy or speech is slurred, more advanced hypothermia is present, and an external heat source is usually needed to help the body rewarm. *Avoid exercise,* as that may bring "after drop": cold blood from the extremities rushes into the body core, with the chance of a heart attack. Likewise, *do not* rub the arms or legs to encourage circulation. Warm baths are fine, but keep the arms and legs out. Hot drinks and alcohol also have been known to produce after drop, so they are best avoided unless the condition is clearly a mild one (shivering is present). Warm compresses on the torso, neck, and head, hot water bottles around these areas inside a sleeping bag, or direct body contact with another person may be required. Use artificial respiration and cardiopulmonary resuscitation (CPR) if necessary.

MARINE TRAFFIC HAZARDS

Some kayakers feel that other boats and ships are as much a danger to paddlers as what nature throws at us. Ships could run down a kayak or upset it in a near miss because of their inability to see it or because they spot it too late for avoidance. Pleasure boats could do the same due to inattention at the helm or even in an attempt to come in for a closer look.

Large ships suffer from two disadvantages. Visibility forward from the ship's bridge is partially obstructed by the hull: from some ships a kayaker is not visible at all when less than a half mile ahead! Also, ships cannot maneuver quickly, and emergency actions, like throwing the engines in reverse (which requires some time to accomplish), are slow to have an effect and may put the ship out of control. Many ships require more than a mile to stop, even with full power astern. Tugs pulling barges are especially unable to change course or to stop quickly.

Consider how small a kayak would appear a mile ahead of a ship's bridge. To get some idea of how visible you are from that ship, imagine your kayak on top of the bridge—probably hardly noticeable—then partially obscure it with whatever waves are around you. The chances that the ship will pick you up on radar are slim. Even if you carried a reflector, it would be too low to the water to produce a significant signal.

The burden is on you to stay out of a ship's path. As with all other pleasure craft, you must stay at least a half mile from approaching ships and a quarter mile aside from passing ones. Fortunately, where they are going is usually quite predictable. The major shipping routes in Puget Sound, Rosario Strait, and the Strait of Juan de Fuca have defined traffic lanes, which are marked in red or purple on nautical charts. Some routes are divided into one-way lanes with a separation zone between the two. Ships are supposed to stay within these lanes. If you can determine where you are in relation to the lane, you can predict where the ship will pass. Though pleasure craft can cross these lanes, they should do so as quickly as possible and otherwise stay out of them. Ships will sometimes deviate from their lane (for example, to pass around a sailboat regatta), so be sure to leave some margin for error for both you and the ship.

Suppose you see a distant ship coming down a traffic lane that you wish to cross. Should you try to cross ahead of it or wait for it to pass? Obviously, the latter is safest, but circumstances do arise when you find yourself needing to proceed ahead to get clear, or when it seems apparent that you can cross ahead safely (slower tugs with tows are especially tempting). Can you make it?

You need to know something about the ship's speed relative to yours, and your respective distances from your crossing point on the traffic lane. Most ships are much faster than they appear—16 knots is typical in our inland waters, though some freighters may move at their full 20-knot sea speed. Tugs with tows average 8 knots, with up to 10 knots possible. Assuming your speed to be 4 knots, ships may be traveling at four to five times that. Make a generous estimate of their speed (using the speeds mentioned) and then compare the ship's distance from where you plan to cross its course to how far you have to go to be clear by a quarter mile on the other side.

Another way to determine what will happen as you approach a ship on a course perpendicular to your own is by watching the ship's position off your bow as you converge. If the interior angle between your bow and the ship's bow gradually increases, that indicates that you will pass the intersection point first (how much sooner is another question). If it stays constant, you are on a collision course; a decreasing angle indicates you will pass astern.

If you find yourself in a situation when you fear you cannot get out of a ship's way, emergency signaling with flares, or with orange smoke in sunny weather, may be your only remedy (though it will probably also bring down upon you the wrath of the Coast Guard, as well as the whole maritime community). The most effective solution is a marine VHF transceiver. Call the ship, let them know what and where you are, and then agree on a solution (do this *before* it is too late for them to take evasive action). Though Channel 16 is the general calling and emergency frequency, ships in Washington's inland waters monitor Channel 14 (Seattle Traffic) or Channel 13 (ships' bridge-to-bridge). If you cannot read the ship's name, call it by position (e.g., "the southbound black container ship off Foulweather Bluff").

For pleasure craft, you will need to rely on visual warnings of your presence, such as a flag attached to a fishing pole if you have a rod holder installed on your deck.

Ferries are a hazard, too. Generally the ferries have much better visibility and maneuverability than ships of comparative size, and they will do their best to go around you. When paddling in groups in narrow channels traversed by ferries (or other traffic for that matter), stay close together and avoid getting strung out across their path. If you are taking evasive action, decide on a direction and stay with it so that the ferry can react accordingly. Be especially cautious around docked ferries. Be sure that they are not about to leave as you cross ahead (give them a wide berth anyhow), and watch out for their prop wash. Paddling underneath ferry docks is both *illegal and dangerous,* as the prop wash from a docking or departing ferry can easily wrap your boat around a piling.

Tides and Currents

In Pacific Northwest waters, staying in tune with tides and tidal currents is as important as keeping an eye on the weather and the marine traffic. Adverse currents can slow or stop your progress, but more important are the hazards of rough water created by currents and possibly made far worse by weather.

Tidal currents (the horizontal movement of water) stem from tides (the vertical movement of water), so paying attention to tide cycles is helpful for picking the safest traveling times.

Tides in the inland waters of the Northwest are generally "mixed semidiurnal," which simply means that there are two daily cycles of high and low tides. Typically, one low is considerably lower than the other, as shown in figure 1. The exact shape of the daily curve changes during the month, and at times the smaller cycle may become little more than an afterthought—just a small deviation in the primary cycle.

The strength of a current is roughly proportionate to the size of the ongoing exchange, or the difference between high and low tide. Thus, in figure 1, the flood current between lower low (l.l.) water and higher high (h.h.) will be swifter than that during the exchange from higher

Fig. 1. A typical daily tide cycle in Puget Sound (h.h. = higher high; h.l. = higher low; l.h. = lower high; l.l. = lower low). The differences between highs and lows, and the order in which the higher and lower highs and lows occur, are in constant flux during the month.

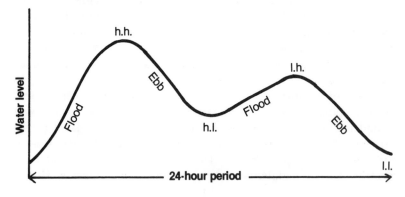

low (h.l.) to lower high (l.h.) later in the day. Since the order of this mixed semidiurnal pattern varies from day to day, the tide graphs included in some tide tables (*Tidelog,* for example—see Useful Publications) are helpful for getting an overview of the day's current strengths.

Another important factor is the duration of exchanges. Though the average time lapse between high tide and low is about six hours, the current-flow interval in some places can be as much as nine hours on very big exchanges or little more than an hour on very small ones (during which there may be hardly any current).

You should also be aware of the bimonthly cycles in tide and current size caused by the alignment of the moon in relation to the earth and the sun. Every 14 days a period of "spring" (nothing to do with the season) tides and bigger-than-usual currents occurs when the moon is either full or new (aligned either between or on the far side of the earth in relation to the sun). In between spring tides are periods of "neap" tides and currents, which are smaller than average, occurring during quarter moons when the moon is out of alignment with the sun and earth. These cycles exert their biggest influence on outer coast tides and currents. They have less effect on inland tides, though they do affect inland currents to some extent.

More important in Northwest inland waters is the declination of the moon's orbit from the equator, which follows 14-day cycles independent of the spring-neap progressions. The difference between the sizes of the two daily tides and their accompanying currents will be greatest when the moon is at its maximum north or south declination. Since the moon's orbit is elliptical, those periods of the month when it is closest to the earth ("perigee") produce larger tides and stronger currents, particularly on the inside waters.

In short, all of these factors can cause dramatic differences in tides and currents, particularly when they coincide. As a consequence, current speeds can be more than twice what they are on another day at the same stage of the tide. So take a close look at your monthly tide tables to keep track of such trends, and note that the two daily cycles are somewhat independent of each other. Many tide and current tables include calendars noting the astronomical conditions so that you can see their effects.

Times of no current are called "slack water" (or, in some documents, "minimum flood or ebb current," because the water may not completely stop flowing). The length of the slack is related to the strength of the currents before and after it. *Slack water times do not necessarily coincide with high or low tide.* The characteristics of each waterway greatly affect the differences between tides and currents. Hence, mariners use current tables to predict slacks and times of maximum current, and these are far more useful for travel planning than tide tables, though kayakers find the latter useful for timing launches and haul-outs.

PREDICTING NORTHWEST CURRENTS

Predictions for tidal currents are found in two types of documents: current tables, and current charts or atlases.

Current tables are available from two sources. The National Oceanic and Atmospheric Administration's *Current Tables for the Pacific Coast of North America and Asia* is a hefty but inexpensive book that gives current predictions for points between San Diego, California, and the Aleutian Islands, and then west to the Philippines. Because of this range, 90 percent of the volume is worthless if you plan to paddle only the area covered in this book. For those who need only local information, the Island Canoe Company publishes a booklet that includes the NOAA tables for both currents and tides for Puget Sound north through the Gulf Islands (see Useful Publications). Like the NOAA volume, it is good for one year. The Canadian Hydrographic Service publishes its own tables (use the green volume for the Gulf Islands), which are very similar in format to the NOAA tables.

Current tables are composed of two parts, which allow predictions of slack water and maximum currents at specific places. The first part is a calendar of times for slack water and maximum current (with speed predicted for that time) for major reference points. In Washington's inland waters, for example, these are Admiralty Inlet, Tacoma Narrows, Deception Pass, Rosario Strait, and San Juan Channel. Following these are correction factors for many local places, based on the major reference points and showing how local currents will differ from those in time and speed. The Appendix includes an example of how these local corrections work for a particular place and time (see Calculating Currents with the NOAA Tables). The Island Canoe Company also publishes two current guides that show the local correction factors at their appropriate places on maps, making them easier to find and use during route planning.

Current charts or *current atlases* show schematic pictures of current flows at different stages of the tide. They are easier to use than current tables and are best for getting an overall picture of the flows during a particular time period when route planning. In some areas such as the San Juan Islands' east/west channels, where flows are far from intuitively obvious, current charts and atlases can be a great help. Another advantage is that these are perennial rather than annual. However, they are less accurate for predicting slack-water times. For places where that is critical, such as Deception Pass, use the current tables.

For Puget Sound, Hood Canal, and Admiralty Inlet NOAA publishes two sets of current charts that are meant to be used in conjunction with the annual current tables. For the San Juan Islands and the Gulf Islands the Canadian Hydrographic Service's *Current Atlas: Juan de Fuca Strait to Strait of Georgia* accurately locates both current streams and the large eddies that occur in this complex area. It also shows how current streams vary both in strength and location depending on the size of the tidal exchange. The major difficulty with this book is finding the right chart to use. To do so, you must have a Canadian tide table and make some calculations about the tide times and exchange size. As an alternative, consult my annual publication, *Washburne's Tables,* which takes you directly to the right chart for any hour of any day without need for tide table, calculations, or daylight saving time corrections.

HAZARDS FROM CURRENTS

The majority of sea-kayaking accidents in the Northwest have resulted at least in part from currents, usually aggravated by bad weather. The most common dangers are those caused by the interaction of wind and currents.

When wind-generated waves encounter an opposing current (one moving against the wind), the waves are slowed down or, if the current is strong enough, prevented from advancing at all. The waves become steeper, larger, and may break heavily. The result is a much rougher and more difficult sea for small craft to handle. A channel that has only moderate seas when the current is flowing in the wind's direction may turn into something untenable for kayaks after the current change.

Consequently, kayakers should plan to cross open water when the current and wind are moving in the same direction. Though the wind direction cannot be anticipated with certainty, currents can. (In nautical publications, wind and current directions customarily are expressed in opposite fashion to each other: winds in the direction from which they are *coming,* but currents in the direction toward which they are *going.*)

In November 1983, a kayaker died while crossing from Tumbo Island in British Columbia to Patos Island in the San Juan Islands, a stretch of water known for its strong currents. Though the 50-knot winds that caught the party in midchannel alone could have caused the fatality, the heavy breaking seas were made worse by a large eddy that resulted in currents contrary to the winds during a time when the general flow was in the wind's direction. This eddy could have been identified only with the Canadian *Current Atlas*. (See *Sea Kayaker* magazine, Spring 1984, for a report of the incident.)

In certain situations, waves are forced to break in quite localized areas, called "tide rips." Most tide rips occur where land obstructions or underwater shoals impede or change the current flow, causing the moving water to accelerate because it is being squeezed around a point, through a narrows, or over a shallows (figure 2). Waves may be able to advance against slower currents up to that place, but when they cannot get farther they expend their energy in breaking, become concentrated and trapped in rips such as at eddy lines, and result in turbulence.

Where currents intersect, they form an eddy line at their edges. If the difference in current speeds is great enough, waves are unable to cross this barrier, and a rip composed of stalled, multidirectional waves forms adjacent to it. The effect is reminiscent of the intersecting waves found near a vertical shoreline where waves are being reflected back through the incoming ones. The waves become irregular and pyramid-shaped, leaping up and disappearing unpredictably. A kayak cannot find an equilibrium on such a rapidly moving surface, so its movement is jerky, you get splashed a lot, and possibly lose your balance and capsize.

Sometimes you encounter rips on calm, windless days. Where do the waves come from? They may stem from very low, widely spaced waves that are barely perceptible until they become trapped and intensified in the tide-rip area. Or, currents flowing over an irregular bottom may be transmitting the bottom features to the surface as standing waves (waves that stay in one place), simply another variety of tide rip. Occasionally rips are the result of a large eddy being swept downstream from the place where it was created, and persisting (with adjacent rips) for quite some time and distance.

The rough water in rips also may be created or intensified by the wakes of ships or even pleasure craft. I have seen very minor rips turn into nasty ones after a powerboat passed by. Ship wakes can make such situations far worse.

It is difficult to predict with certainty where rips will be located even if you know the direction and speed of currents; there is just too little information on charts about bottom features. However, the downstream sides of points or islands (particularly those surrounded by shallows), shoaling areas, underwater reefs, places where currents are fastest or currents intersect (such as where they rejoin after flowing around a large island) are all good candidates. In the San Juan Islands, for instance, colliding currents from Spieden Channel and San Juan Channel regularly form dangerous rips. The particularly fast water at

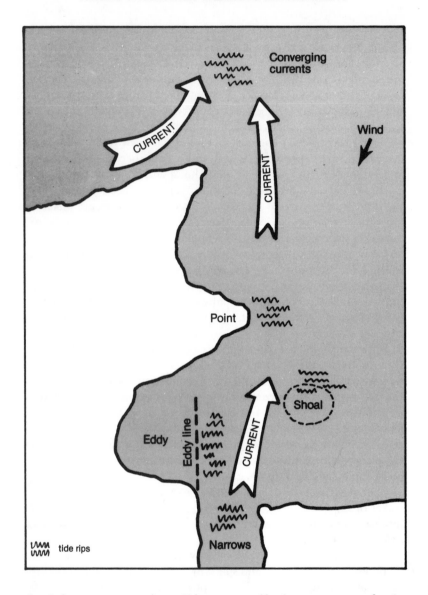

Fig. 2. Situations causing tide rips. Tide rips are possible wherever a current is forced to change speed or direction or where currents converge. Wind is not necessary for rips to form, but generally it makes them much worse.

San Juan Channel's south entrance usually has rips, which are at their worst on ebbs against southerly winds.

From a distance, tide rips can be heard as a low roar. Seeing them from the low viewing point of a kayak is harder, particularly on windy days when distant rips are camouflaged by wind waves. If you find yourself heading for a rip, assess your drift in the current and then try to take evasive action while there is still time. Determining your direction of drift can be done with ranges: compare something in the middle ground (a buoy or a rock) to a feature in the background (a hill or tree), and observe their movement in relation to each other. Frequent checking of two ranges at right angles to each other (one ahead and one to the side) will help keep track of what the current is doing to you and how effective your paddling is in countering it.

If you cannot avoid the rip, head straight through it. Remember that you are moving with the current, whereas the rip is stationary, and you will soon pass through it. With most rips, there is more noise and splashing than real threat to your stability. I prefer to paddle rapidly, each stroke serving as a minibrace to help maintain my equilibrium and direction.

Often, when a current passes along an irregular shoreline or around a point, the flow breaks off from the main current near shore, forming an eddy of still water or even a back eddy—water moving in the opposite direction of the current for a short distance. Such eddies usually form on the downstream side of points, islets, or other obstructions. Sometimes the eddy system will extend out alongside the obstruction as well. Sharply defined eddy lines between the moving water in the current and the still or backward-flowing water in the eddy are often accompanied by swirls, turbulence, or even whirlpools. The southeast side of Pass Island in Deception Pass on a strong flood current is a good example of this situation.

Eddy lines can sometimes upset small craft, including kayaks. The primary cause is inertia: crossing from current to eddy or vice versa involves a rapid transition into water going a different direction. Consequently, the rule is to lean and brace *downstream*. Also, the tremendous turbulence and up- and down-welling in some eddy lines can focus strong torquing forces on a kayak's hull, possibly causing you to capsize.

Crossing powerful eddy lines is best done quickly and at right angles. Keep paddling at a rapid pace so that strokes can serve as braces. Crossing through weaker eddy lines is discussed on the following page.

USING EDDIES TO GO UPSTREAM

Usually, wherever currents are found, there also are eddies along the shore made up of either still water or localized currents moving upstream for some distance. The more irregular the shoreline, the more extensive the eddy system. A good example is San Juan Island's shore along Spieden Channel. During one strong spring-tide ebb, I and a group of young campers in canoes easily traversed this shoreline via its eddy system, while in midchannel two sailboats going the same way stood stationary under both sail and power. We had long since rounded Limestone Point and gone our separate ways by the time the sailors had pulled themselves out of the current's grasp.

The boundaries between the main current stream and an eddy may be marked by turbulence or changes in the texture of the water's surface, which may be difficult to see in slower currents. Within the eddy itself, which may cover an extensive area, water can move in many different directions. Most eddies are actually circling water. I usually move around as I progress through large eddies to find the most favorable currents, using cues such as the direction in which the kelp lies.

More than likely, you will be forced to paddle hard to progress upstream from one eddy to the next, usually when you must round a point where, for a short distance, the current sweeps along the shore as fast as in midstream. Such "eddy hopping" requires some positioning, careful boat handling, and perhaps a burst of everything you have for a short, hard pull. Use the still water generally found just downstream from a point to build up some speed and inertia, then break out into the opposing current as far upstream and as close to the point as possible. Head as directly upstream as possible as you enter the main current; otherwise the boat's bow will be pushed out and you will find yourself heading perpendicular to where you intended to go, rapidly losing ground. If this occurs, rather than trying to recover, just continue to turn downstream, reenter the eddy you just left, and try again.

Going Ashore

Kayakers are amphibious creatures, at home on both sea and land, and able to make the transition easily and frequently. In many other parts of the country, going ashore often puts you in somebody's front yard or private preserve. By contrast, the Pacific Northwest is well endowed with public lands hospitable to boaters.

Many of the trips listed in this book are two days long or more, so you will need some camping gear and outdoor skills for these. Though this book offers no primer on camping, a few peculiarities of kayak camping along these inland waters are worth noting, including things that kayakers can do to minimize their effects on these wildlands and their wildlife while ashore or paddling nearby.

PUBLIC SHORELANDS

Most public lands are available for use by everyone, but some (particularly national wildlife refuges) are not. Following is a brief description of the different jurisdictions and what kayakers can expect in each.

National Parks. Washington has one national park on its inland shoreline: San Juan Island National Historic Park, commemorating the so-called Pig War of 1859 between Britain and the United States. There are two units, both on San Juan Island: American Camp at the southern end and British Camp on the northwest side. The park has historical reconstructions and interpretive programs, and facilities for picnicking but not for camping. (The National Park Service avoids providing camping facilities where neighboring agencies can do it, as is the case in the San Juan Islands.) Camping is not allowed on the park's undeveloped lands.

National Wildlife Refuges. The Nisqually, San Juan Islands, and Dungeness national wildlife refuges all control shorelines along Washington's inside waters. The Nisqually and Dungeness refuges allow boating close to shore and walking onshore as long as nesting sites are not disturbed. Areas may be closed during sensitive times of year. The San Juan Islands refuge includes almost all of the small islets, rocks, and reefs in that area, and some larger islands such as Flattop, Skipjack, and Smith islands. Many of these are also part of the National Wilderness Preservation System. No landings are allowed on any of these 80-odd places without permission of the U.S. Fish and Wildlife Service, which requests that you stay at least 200 yards from these refuge islands. Such islands are particularly inviting to kayakers, but this is a case of protecting birds' and seals' rights to peaceful nesting and haul outs, and the U.S. Fish and Wildlife Service will not compromise these goals to provide public recreation. Where units of the San Juan Islands refuge are encountered on routes in this book, you will be cautioned to keep away from them. They are well marked with signs to that effect. Two islands in the refuge, Matia Island and Turn Island, have portions leased to the Washington State Parks Department. You may camp in these park areas and walk the trails on the rest of the islands or land on most of the beaches as long as birds' nesting sites are not nearby.

Washington State Parks. State parks provide the most extensive opportunities for both day use and camping throughout Washington's inland waterways. Although most of Washington's park sites are developed, some of the marine (boat access only) state parks are totally undeveloped and overnight camping is not permitted. However, with a few exceptions, camping is allowed at the many small island parks where sanitation (a pit toilet) is provided. Most of these also have picnic tables and fire rings, but no drinking water. Examples of such undeveloped camping sites are Blind Island, McMicken Island, and Posey Island state parks. There is no camping fee, largely because it is too much trouble to collect it.

Aside from these small islands, most marine state parks charge a fee, which is collected through self-registration stations. These fees may not be in effect between October and April, though the schedule varies from park to park. A few state parks with more highly developed campgrounds are popular with kayakers. These developed sites (usually with bathrooms with running water) charge more, but some parks also have a few less developed sites near the water for boaters at a lower fee (consult the ranger). Examples are Jarrell Cove and Spencer Spit state parks.

Dispersed camping (that is, establishing your own campsite in the woods) is not permitted in any of Washington's state parks. This is to prevent spreading the impact that camping has on wildlands. It is also to avoid conflicts with other management goals, such as eagle habitat management in the San Juan Islands.

Be prepared to take your trash home with you. Many marine state parks now have a pack-it-out garbage program to combat the high cost of removing the mountains of trash deposited by boaters on the island parks.

British Columbia Marine Provincial Parks. Policies and facilities are comparable to those of Washington's state parks, with "full-service" campgrounds used by kayakers in the Gulf Islands at Montague Harbor and Sidney Spit. Other island parks have a much lower development level (a few have hand pumps for drinking water), and some have none. Camping is generally allowed, though fires are prohibited unless an official fireplace is provided and no fire bans are in effect.

Washington Department of Natural Resources (DNR) Recreation Areas. The Department of Natural Resources manages some of the best-kept secrets along Washington shorelines, primarily because they are not labeled on most nautical charts. The DNR's recreation areas are picnic and camp sites that provide most of the same amenities that state parks provide, but without a fee for their use. Facilities are simple (pit toilets, usually no water), and maintenance is infrequent, as the DNR covers a large area with a tiny staff. (Ironically, as of this writing, the DNR still provides and empties trash cans at most sites.)

Even less well-known are DNR "school lands." These usually undeveloped parcels are managed to provide income (usually from timber) for local schools, hence the name. The DNR has no objection to public recreation, even camping, as long as fires are not built. These parcels are identified on DNR maps (see Useful Publications).

The DNR also manages the state's public tidelands, which are scattered throughout Puget Sound and the San Juan Islands (more than half of the tidelands in the latter are public, but few in Hood Canal are). Public tidelands are rarely identified by signs, but booklets and maps showing their locations are available from the DNR (see Useful Publications). Almost all of the public tidelands extend only as high as the mean high-tide line unless the uplands are publicly owned too, so I do not feel these are very useful for kayakers except for a quick leg stretch or some clam digging. Remember, you will be trespassing if you wander above the high-tide line.

CAMPING

Water. To be surrounded by water without a drop to drink is the Ancient Mariner's dilemma. It is shared by sea kayakers who are unfamiliar with camping along Northwest inland waters. The majority of campsites along these shores have no drinking water, and those that do (Jones Island State Park, for example) often run out of it midway through the summer, or shut it off between fall and spring.

Unless you are going somewhere where you know there will be water, carry your own. Take along enough to tide you over should you have to stay longer because of bad weather (so you won't be forced to beg water from yachts or head for home in dangerous conditions.)

Three quarts per person per day usually is enough if you are careful with it. Wash dishes in salt water (followed by a sparing rinse with fresh water to prevent corrosion) and add it to fresh water for cooking. A half-and-half combination is about right for water that will be poured off (such as for boiling noodles), and one part salt water to two or more parts fresh water is a good ratio when the water stays in the food (such as in cooking rice).

A collapsible two- to three-gallon jug fits well in most kayaks. A larger number of smaller water bottles, however, are easier to fit in a small boat, provide better trim, and give better protection against water leaking away.

Fires and Stoves. Though most public campsites have fire rings or grates, firewood is not always available. In most places, driftwood is the only option, and during the busy months all the small pieces have been collected. Bring a saw and a hatchet or an ax. I prefer to carry a backpacking stove to do my cooking, and I build a fire only for warmth or the aesthetic value.

Beach fires generally are not allowed, both because of the unsightly scars they leave and because they can get out of control and spread to the uplands. Wildfires are a particular fear in drier places such as the San Juan and Gulf islands during the summer, so build fires only in designated rings and never leave them unattended.

For comfortable camping during the off-season, I find a larger tent heated with a small wood stove makes the difference between tolerable existence and real pleasure. My winter shelter is a floorless nylon wall tent modified by adding a hole and pocket for the stovepipe flange in the end wall. A woven polypropylene tarp covers the floor away from the stove. Wood stoves small enough to fit in a kayak are available commercially (both folding or rigid models). I make my own out of two-gallon gas cans or from sheet metal; these fit behind my seat in the kayak and last about one season. The flue consists of two sections of either two-inch galvanized (not aluminum) gutter downspout, or three-inch stovepipe. The two pipe elbows store inside the stove. Setting the stove up on a few rocks leaves almost no trace from its heat after the tent is removed.

Raccoons. Cuteness is the sole virtue of the ubiquitous raccoon (*Larcenus pestiferens*). You can expect a visit from these bold and persistent critters at any time, day or night. Their ability to cart off large food packages is notorious.

James Island State Park is home for the commando elite of raccoons, well known for their bravado and larcenous skills, which they continuously hone on park visitors. The tenacity and deviousness of this cadre is unequaled in all the San Juan Islands. They never desist from their mission and apparently never sleep. Neither will you. I recall one winter's night when their persistent efforts to liberate my food from my tent, where I lay clutching it, reduced me to chasing them through the bushes in my underwear with a flashlight, dementedly determined to drive them all into the sea. I failed.

Hanging food is protection only if done cleverly enough to foil these excellent climbers. Another solution, if you have a double kayak, is to store food in the large plastic jars in which Greek olives are shipped (these are too big for the average single boat). Reportedly raccoon-proof, these jars have large screw lids, and one will hold several days' worth of food. You can usually buy them at Greek restaurants and delicatessens.

A final note to aid a half-decent night's sleep: bring everything that clanks or rattles (cookware, etc.) into the tent with you, or suffer through listening to the raccoons examining it all night.

Solitude. An important ingredient to satisfactory camping, solitude may be the most difficult to find during the summer months and particularly on major holidays. I spent one Memorial Day weekend sleeping on the beach at Sucia Island, because all the campsites were occupied. During such peak times, try to aim for places less attractive to overnight boaters: sites without docks, moorings, or protected anchorages. Look to some of the lesser-known DNR sites, especially those with no overland access and poor landings for boats.

Another major impact on solitude in the San Juans is the canoeing and kayaking groups from YMCA Camp Orkila (pronounced Or-KIY-la) on Orcas Island. There may be as many as five groups of a dozen or so youngsters each on the water and camping throughout the San Juan Islands at any one time. Fortunately, they do have a fixed schedule of campsites, so you can arrange to avoid them by calling the camp: (206) 382-5009 in Seattle, or (206) 376-2678 on Orcas Island.

MINIMUM IMPACT

Though the effect of each sea kayaker is minimal, there are now enough of us that some problem patterns are emerging and will increase with kayaking's popularity unless each of us is aware of the impact on the environment.

Marine mammals (particularly seals) and birds are most vulnerable when they are bearing and rearing their young. Mother seals may abandon their pups if they become separated from them or if the pups are handled by humans. Seal pups do not know enough to fear humans, and there have been reports of pups trying to climb aboard kayaks! Stay clear of mothers with young and paddle away from pups if they approach you.

Birds are particularly sensitive when they are incubating their eggs. (The incubation period varies from species to species.) Bald eagles are of special concern to wildlife managers, as they may abandon their eggs if there is too much human activity in the vicinity of the nest (a major reason that camping is either prohibited or confined to one area in popular eagle-nesting areas such as Patos Island). Eagles are incubating between late March and late May, so be especially unobtrusive on shore or while paddling along shore in eagle country at that time.

Another problem is independent camping in nondesignated sites. One state park ranger told me: "Sea kayakers used to be my favorite user group, but now they're becoming a problem. Too many of them

Loading up on the west beach at Jones Island

like to find their own campsite in the woods, and even though they are careful about fires and what they leave behind, they tell their friends about it, and soon I've got another well-established illegal campsite."

The problem is that Washington's coastline is simply too popular to provide the isolated camping that many kayakers seek. For that, you simply must head north into British Columbia or find it in the mountains without your kayak. There are opportunities for legal independent camping on undeveloped DNR lands and in some B.C. parks, but they are rare and often not very attractive. (Do not build fires if you camp on these lands.)

We kayakers can cultivate our own interests by being the most inexpensive and inoffensive user group. Support the pack-it-out garbage programs and avoid using the garbage cans that are provided if you can take it home. Stick to designated campsites, and when in doubt, ask.

Going Paddling

This chapter contains information to consider when you prepare for a kayak outing, such as how to evaluate whether your physical condition and skills are appropriate for the trip you have in mind, and whether the distances are appropriate for the time you have as well as the amount of energy you are willing to put out. It also contains general information about launch sites, carrying kayaks onto the ferries as a foot passenger, and some thoughts about paddling during the off-season on these inland waters.

TRIP PLANNING

Nautical Charts. Charts of Washington (issued by NOAA) and British Columbia waters (issued by the Canadian Hydrographic Service) are sold by many nautical-supply retailers around the region. Which chart covers any particular area in Washington is shown in *Nautical Chart Catalog 2: United States, Pacific Coast,* a free brochure available wherever the charts are sold. Canada has a similar index for the Pacific Coast.

Two and sometimes three chart alternatives, with different scales of coverage, are available for any locality in this area. The least-expensive coverage is 1:80,000 charts, available in large, single sheets or in folios containing three sheets printed on lighter paper. The folios are called small craft (SC) charts, and three of them (NOAA's 18423 SC and 18445 SC, and the Canadian Hydrographic Service's 3310) cover all the waters discussed in this book. The detail at this scale is adequate (the Canadian one is better, at 1:40,000) for cruising, and the light paper and small pages make them easy to fold into a chart case. These small craft charts are usually more thorough in identifying parks than the single-sheet equivalents.

Larger-scale charts (such as 1:25,000) give you a more intimate and detailed view of the shorelines, but are more expensive and bulkier, resulting in more frequent turning and refolding. Though I prefer scales of 1:40,000 or larger for the wilder shores of British Columbia and Alaska in order to spot good landing sites, I find the 1:80,000 charts barely adequate but serviceable in Washington. In Washington and southern B.C., land ownership is more relevant to getting ashore than shoreline composition and foreshore extent (the area between high and low tide, which shows how far you might have to carry your boat if the tide is out).

Daily Distance. The distance you cover on a daily basis depends on how much time you are willing to spend in the boat. This factor is far more important than your paddling strength or the boat's speed. In general, most people cruise at between 3 or 4 knots (nautical miles per hour). With stops to look around, rest, or stretch my legs, I average about 2 knots for the day as a whole (time between getting under way in the morning and hauling out for the evening divided by miles traveled). Ten nautical miles per day seems a comfortable distance for most people in average paddling conditions (barring strong head winds). Using the current can make a dramatic difference. A group of us once clocked ourselves at 5 knots over a 10-mile distance of fairly leisurely paddling with a favorable current.

Weather Allowances and Alternative Routes. One of the most dangerous situations into which kayakers get themselves is *having* to be someplace at a certain time. This self-induced pressure prompts them to paddle during unsettled weather in exposed places. For some trips I have included route options, which offer safer but longer ways back to your launch point or to somewhere from which you could hitch a ride back to your car. The existence of such options is incorporated in the trip ratings for this book.

The more exposed the route and the fewer route options there are, the more time should be allowed for bad weather contingencies. How much depends on the time of year and the regional weather pattern at the time. A large, stable high-pressure area over the Northwest in July probably holds the least likelihood of being weather-bound. In January, however, weather patterns are too changeable to count on forecasted conditions for even a day in advance. During the summer months, you may want to consider the forecast for the period you will be paddling and choose a trip rating accordingly. During the off-season, periods of bad weather should be assumed. Either build extra time into the itinerary or choose less exposed trips. (Because of the increased hazard potential between September and May, all trip ratings in this book should be considered one rating more hazardous during that time.)

CHOOSING A TRIP

New sea kayakers have difficulty identifying trips where the conditions are within their paddling limits. Saltwater trips are more difficult to classify than those on rivers where conditions can be predicted quite accurately. The water can be mirror smooth on the best of days, and a raging sea in the worst of conditions. There is no sure way to avoid the latter. Overconfidence comes easily on those glassy days, and many sea kayakers have gotten more than they bargained for by taking on challenging routes after better-than-average weather on early trips. It is wise to start out slowly and experience a range of weather conditions in protected situations before testing your skills in more exposed places.

TRIP RATINGS

I have rated the trips primarily on the potential for trouble from either weather or currents, and on the availability of "escape" routes. These ratings take into account the amount of protection provided by land in windy conditions, and the distance from shore that paddling each route requires. The ratings also consider currents and the hazards they can introduce, and hazards from marine shipping traffic. Daily paddling distances (determined by either a minimum loop distance, or the least distance between campsites) may be longer for trips with a more challenging rating.

Even the lowest rating presumes some kayak experience—*no* saltwater trip is recommended for your first time in a kayak. A first-time kayaker should start by learning basic boat-handling skills in a pool and then in lake water (which is likely to be warmer and smoother than the inland seas).

These ratings are effective from late spring through early fall. *Each trip moves up one rating during the off-season,* October through April (see Paddling During the Off-season later in this chapter).

A trip designated as "Protected" is suitable for novice kayakers possessing basic boat-handling skills and rudimentary familiarity with nautical charts. Daily distances are 7 miles or less. Routes mostly follow the shore, with no crossings over 1 mile. Waters are largely protected by nearby landforms, and sea currents never exceed 1 knot. Tide rips are unlikely.

A trip designated as "Moderate" is suitable for kayakers who have well-established boat-handling skills, who have some previous saltwater paddling experience, are aware of current and weather patterns, and can use current- and weather-prediction resources for planning. Since this rating may commit you to paddling in wind and choppy seas, you should be able to stay on course and keep upright through balance and bracing in these conditions. Daily distances may be up to 10 miles on waters where crossings of 1 mile or more are required, and wind and current could cause dangerous seas. You may need to cross marine shipping lanes. Currents may attain 2 knots or so for short distances, and tide rips are possible, especially in opposing wind conditions. "Moderate + " indicates the presence of a localized hazard that can be avoided by timing your travel or by choosing an alternate route.

A trip designated as "Exposed" is suitable for experienced sea kayakers who have a thorough understanding of weather and currents and their interaction, and who can handle their boats in rough water. The potential for very rough seas is greater on these routes, and long open-water crossings may require paddling for some time in these conditions. You may need to cross major marine shipping lanes. Daily distances may be 10 miles or more, with travel in exposed seas 1 mile or more from the nearest shore. Currents may exceed 2 knots, and tide rips are likely. Trips of this class become very risky during the off-season and should be undertaken only with ample buffer time to await safe weather.

KAYAKS AND FERRIES

Both the Washington and British Columbia ferry systems allow foot passengers to carry kayaks aboard (preferably on a cart or dolly). Washington charges the motorcycle rate for the boat, and B.C. charges the bicycle rate. This results in significant cost savings to the single paddler who leaves the car at the ferry dock. At least in Washington, a couple with two kayaks car-topped on one vehicle can save money by driving on. In the San Juan Islands and for Vashon Island, the round-trip fee structure (collected on the mainland) means a free ride if you paddle out to the island(s) and ferry back.

The savings are not as significant as the flexibility that carrying a kayak on board allows in choosing paddling routes. For example, you can have a fine day excursion paddling from Winslow to Bremerton if you use the Seattle-Winslow and Bremerton-Seattle ferries to start and finish (see the Winslow to Bremerton chapter). In the San Juans and Gulf islands, you can leave your car on the mainland, ferry to one island stop, paddle to another, amd ferry or paddle back to the car. In the San Juans, for instance, you could park your car at the Anacortes terminal, ride to Shaw Island, paddle to Friday Harbor, and then ride back.

Carrying a kayak on board also provides a significant bad weather fallback, particularly in the San Juan and Gulf islands, where paddling to a closer or less exposed terminal and ferrying may be safer than paddling back to your car, wherever it is parked.

During the summer months, large numbers of foot passengers with kayaks make the San Juan Islands ferry run particularly hectic. The ferry staff recommends a few things to make it easier for everyone.

First, arrive at least one hour early. This will give you time to find parking and to get your boat and gear ready to board. The biggest problem that carry-on kayaks pose for the ferry staff is the multiple trips that kayakers make to get their gear aboard, which delays loading cars. They ask that you consolidate as much as possible and/or use a boat cart to minimize the trips.

Because of the tremendous growth in use of the San Juan Islands ferries in recent years—and because walk-on kayak traffic has increased most dramatically—kayaks now compete with cars for spaces on the ferries. Westbound from Anacortes, the crews are able to fit kayaks into "void spaces" (those not used by other vehicles) well enough that kayaks readied for boarding ahead of time will stand a good chance of getting aboard, at least at this writing. But eastbound from the islands, these void spaces cannot be filled readily. Since each island has an allotment of vehicle spaces on each ferry, kayaks must be counted into these and wait their turn to fill them. You will not be required to line up with the cars; kayaks can be staged near the ramp.

Kayakers who carry on their boats need a put-in within walking distance of the ferry terminal where they disembark. In almost all cases, there is someplace to do that, but at some there may be a fee for the privilege. They are described in trips that involve those ferry terminals.

LAUNCHING AND PARKING

Finding a place to launch your kayak and leave your car while you are gone can be something of a problem. Some shorelines are well endowed with public facilities providing both access to the water and convenient parking. Others, particularly in certain parts of the San Juan Islands, are limited in public shore access or parking areas, or both. Orcas Island has the least public access and parking, and private property is the probable option—at a cost.

In researching this book, I encountered bad feelings about kayakers among Orcas Island residents. Their sentiments have nothing to do with kayakers on the water, only with kayakers getting to the water. One waterfront resident reported finding two kayakers sorting out gear on her lawn in preparation for launching. A marina owner found five kayakers loading their boats on his float, preempting spaces for boats stopping to shop in his store. Another islander summed up her feelings this way: "I identify with kayakers and why they come here and know they appreciate the same things about the islands that I do. But some of them act like the whole place is a park, where they have a right to everything at no cost to themselves. They take, but give nothing back; they rarely buy anything in the stores like other boaters do. When they expect to use our property too, that's the last straw!"

Such bad feelings are certainly not in kayakers' best interests, particularly since it is the nature of our means of travel to interact more with people along the way than most other boaters do. The situation is easily redressed when attention is paid to both our actions and attitudes.

First, we should overcome our reluctance to buy locally, even if prices are a bit higher. If possible, buy food locally. Expect to pay for launching or parking privileges on private land. (For each of the trips in this book originating on Orcas Island, I have listed private launching/parking sites as well as public ones.) Most important, *ask* before using any private land, even if there aren't any NO TRESPASSING signs.

On Shaw Island, there have been conflicts with the Franciscan nuns who operate the ferry dock and the adjoining general store. The nuns complain that kayakers snarl vehicle traffic at the landing and use their floats east of the ferry dock for launching. Until recently, they contested kayakers' access to the beach just west of the landing, which has since been determined to be a public right-of-way. This is a fine launch point for carry-on kayaks, but avoid parking a car there. Get your boats and gear down to the beach as quickly as possible to avoid congestion of the area near the store (which carries all sorts of provisions appealing to kayakers).

Finally, before we leave this topic, I strongly suggest that you avoid Waldron Island entirely in your San Juan Islands travels. Enough unfortunate incidents involving kayakers have occurred there to prompt the residents' council to formally protest to the state about attracting boating use to the island through the DNR's tideland publications. Be advised that, other than public tidelands, there are no public beaches, toilets, or parklands, and that you are *not* welcome to visit there. Please paddle elsewhere.

PADDLING DURING THE OFF-SEASON

For me, paddling in Northwest inland waters during the off-season is just as appealing as during the summer. In fact, there is much about it that I prefer.

During the winter months, there are fewer boats with which to share the waterways. A quiet wildness comes from the scarcity of boats, and from having whole marine park islands to yourself as you would never expect in your wildest dreams of summer. Other boaters met are kindred spirits who appreciate the advantages of winter boating to the extent that they are foolish enough to be out there, too. Boaters are more inclined to say a few words as they pass one another, acknowledging some sort of bond.

Then there are the many seabird species that are rarely seen in the warmer summer months. There are the overcast November days, when the air and the sea are languid, almost paralyzed, from dawn to dusk. Silence is broken only by the distant conversations of floating seabirds or the gentle breathing of a passing harbor porpoise.

The question of imminent weather is seldom far from the winter paddler's mind. Winter in these waters is a stern, no-nonsense time of year. You do things on nature's terms or suffer the consequences.

The changeability and strength of the winds during the winter months are major hazards to contend with. Upgrading the trips to a more severe rating for the off-season is entirely justified for this reason alone.

Weather is simply more unpredictable during the off-season. Fronts and low-pressure systems follow each other in much closer succession. Conditions are more extreme and changeable. And you must paddle in rougher and more uncertain situations than you might prefer. As you move along, there is also the pressure of time: twilight lurks never far away. With the stronger winds and the more fully developed seas, tide rips can occur where they rarely do in less windy times. And those admittedly reassuring passing pleasure craft that, during the summer, were eagerly watching for the chance to rescue you are now snug in their moorings, while winter wilderness isolation is all yours.

I recall one trip from Lopez Island to James Island through Thatcher Pass on an unsettled November day. It bore little resemblance to the placid summer "pond" across which I had lazed my way countless times before. Winds gusted from one direction, settled to flat calm, shifted, and blew hard out of another direction in the space of an hour. Rips popped up where I had never seen them before. The daylight faded far too soon, and through it all, there was nary another boat to be seen.

Other memorable moments of kayak terror have taken place in the winter. The seas may not have been significantly bigger than those of the summer, but there was frequently the fear of a medium sea about to become a nasty one, when I became aware of the chill of the splashes on my hands and face and how distant the shore suddenly seemed.

There are other differences in the winter. Beaches, particularly gravel ones, become steeper. The characteristically bigger waves tend to move the beach material more, piling it up at the current water level so that there is a definite berm or steep drop-off. The consequences are two. First, launching or landing may result in a raised bow on the beach and the stern in the water, a precarious position that often terminates in a spill. Second, a "dumping" surf, one that abruptly releases its energy close to shore, may hinder entering or exiting the boat.

One January morning a friend and I launched at Clark Island into a heavy chop coming across Rosario Strait. Because of the surf on the beach, we each buttoned up in our boats before launching and paddle-poling ourselves off the steep, slippery beach. I slithered out with no problem, but the sharp stern of my friend's kayak buried itself in the steep berm, leaving him teetering precariously in the surf until he could lever himself off with his paddle.

Daily wind patterns from the summer no longer hold either, particularly the axiom of least wind in early morning. These summer cycles are largely generated by the heating of land masses and consequent convection currents. But the low angle of the sun in the winter gives it far less heating power, and the land often remains as cold or colder than the sea, generating little convection.

Next to weather, the biggest constraint on paddling during the off-season is the short daylight. Kayakers need a relatively long time between getting up in the morning and getting under way. In comparing notes with others, I find that two hours is about the standard.

Hence, during the shortest days of the year, trying to make 10 miles a day requires using every minute of daylight. If you hate rising before dawn (as I do) and it gets light at 8:00 A.M., that means getting on the water at 10:00 A.M. Assuming about 2 knots for travel speed and a brief lunch stop, you should plan to reach your next camp at about 3:00 P.M., with an hour of fading light left in which to get ashore and set up camp. I am particularly wary of being caught on the water at dusk in the winter, since a quick change of weather (for the worse) in the dark is especially unnerving and dangerous.

Off-season camping likewise requires the acceptance of some austerities in return for your own private reserve of gorgeous winter wildlands—perhaps bartering an evening under cover in a continuous downpour for a frosty morning walk along a marine park pathway that shows no recent footprints. And for me, the challenge of trying to set up a warm and comfortable evening's nest in spite of what is going on outside is a large part of the season's appeal. My large tent with its wood stove makes all the difference for me at these times of year.

Clothing for the off-season should be able to shed water and wind. With the heavier precipitation and stronger winds, you will want to wear a paddle jacket most of the time. A good barrier against the substantially greater wind-chill factor (even in light breezes) is important for your safety as well as comfort. Some paddlers wear dry suits, though they find them too warm for summer paddling. Gloves that guard against both wetness and cold air are also important. I have found that pogies offer the most effective protection without cramping paddling style.

The west shore of Blake Island

South Puget Sound

Squaxin Island

Squaxin Island State Park is the most popular paddling destination in the South Sound—it provides overnight camping, yet is close enough to launch points on both the east and west sides of Puget Sound for a day trip, using the Boston Harbor or Peale Passage routes described here, respectively. Squaxin Island can be incorporated into a multiday circumnavigation of nearby Hartstene Island, with other overnight camping possibilities at McMicken Island (see the McMicken Island chapter) or Jarrell Cove state parks.

DURATION: Full day or overnight.

RATING: Moderate or Moderate +. The Boston Harbor route requires an open-water crossing and exposure to possible tide rips in Dana Passage. Currents on the Peale Passage route may exceed 1.5 knots at times.

NAVIGATION AIDS: NOAA charts 18445 SC or 18448 (both 1:80,000). Chart 18456 (1:20,000) covers the Boston Harbor route. Use current tables for The Narrows with adjustments for Dana Passage on the Boston Harbor route, or with adjustments for Peale Passage on that route.

PLANNING CONSIDERATIONS: Use the current tables to avoid maximum flows in Dana Passage on the Boston Harbor route. On the Peale Passage route, travel to Squaxin Island on the ebb and return with the flood current.

Getting There and Launching

This area sits astride a portion of Puget Sound where island destinations are separated by only a few miles of water—easily accessible by boat, hours apart by highway. Residents of the west side of Puget Sound can start from the Hartstene Island bridge launch site near Shelton and paddle the Peale Passage route. Those coming from the east will find Boston Harbor near Olympia most convenient.

To reach the Hartstene Island bridge, turn onto Pickering Road from Highway 3 about 8 miles north of Shelton (there is a sign for Hartstene Island). Follow this road approximately 5 miles to the bridge. The

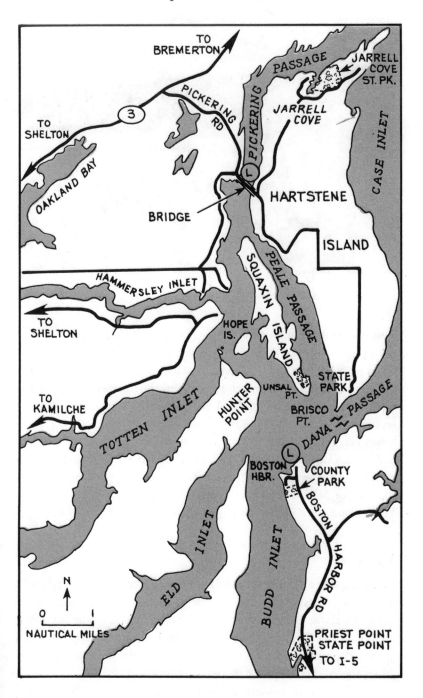

On the beach at Squaxin Island

county's public ramp, dock, and parking lot are located just north of the bridge's western end, with parking for about 20 vehicles.

To reach Boston Harbor, take Exit 105B (Plum Street) from Interstate 5 in Olympia. Drive north after exiting the freeway; the rest of the route is essentially straight ahead. After passing through several intersections for approximately 1 mile, you will see water on the left. Plum Street becomes East Bay Drive, which eventually becomes Boston Harbor Road. Continue another 7 miles to the 73rd Avenue Northeast and turn left. The ramp and parking lot are 0.25 mile beyond, next to Boston Harbor Marina. The paved parking lot across the street is public. The marina store carries basic lunch and snack items.

Routes

Peale Passage (Hartstene Island Bridge to Squaxin Island): *Moderate.* One-way distance is 5 miles. Currents can exceed 1.5 knots along this route. Using favorable currents can make a significant difference for travel, although along-shore eddies can be used to travel against the currents in most places. Tide rips are possible, especially when the current opposes the wind direction.

The flood currents coming around both sides of Hartstene Island meet in the vicinity of northern Squaxin Island. Hence, the flood current flows south from the Hartstene Island bridge (and can be quite strong under the bridge); in Peale Passage the ebb flows in that direction. To make the best use of the currents along the route, start from the bridge about an hour before the turn to the ebb as predicted in the current tables for northern Peale Passage. Return from Squaxin Island State Park about two hours before the turn to the ebb at the same place, so as to ride the flood up Peale Passage and then the new ebb the remainder of the distance. Timing should be about the same for a return via Squaxin Passage and the west side of Squaxin Island.

South of the bridge, the shores in Pickering Passage alternate between houses and steep tree-lined banks, but the shore of Squaxin Island, in Peale Passage, is a fine oasis of natural beauty. Paddling close to its shore, you can imagine yourself exploring Puget Sound two centuries ago with British explorer Captain George Vancouver. With the exception of the state park, Squaxin Island is an Indian reservation. *Do not go ashore without permission.* Squaxin's east shore has escaped development except for an oyster-rearing operation in the bay midway down the island. Occasional decaying shacks are the only signs of the island's sparse settlement. More evident residents are river otter, blue heron, or even a coyote trotting along the beach.

Squaxin Island State Park has a dock at the mouth of the shallow cove, and ample campsites in a strip of lawn that extends along the beach to the south for about 0.25 mile. All sites provide easy access for boats and gear, and those farthest from the dock are likely to offer the most privacy. Solar composting toilets are available. Drinking water is not provided at this park. A camping fee is collected through a self-registration station near the dock.

Boston Harbor to Squaxin Island: *Moderate +.* The one-way distance is about 3 miles. According to local park rangers, this is a very popular trip for people trying kayaks for the first time, with potentially disastrous results. Dana Passage currents can attain almost 3 knots at times, and rips can be lively here, especially with an opposing wind.

The strongest currents can be avoided by crossing directly from Boston Harbor to Squaxin Island. This route, however, involves crossing 2 miles of open water. Also, an ebb current flows southeast from Unsal Point on Squaxin Island most of the time, averaging a little over 1 knot at its peak, making this route most practical for the return.

Because of the opposing current and the uncertainties of a longer open crossing during unsettled weather, the Dana Passage route may be the preferred way north to Squaxin Island, if you take precautions with the Dana Passage currents. Follow close to the shore east from Boston Harbor, and then cross Dana Passage to Brisco Point on Hartstene Island when currents are slack or at least flowing in the same direction as the wind. Then follow Hartstene Island's west shore north to opposite Squaxin Island State Park before crossing.

McMicken Island

Located along the eastern shore of Hartstene Island, this little state park is a low-key destination that can be accessed easily from Tacoma or the Bremerton area via the Key Peninsula. It is a potential overnight stop for a multiday circumnavigation of Hartstene Island. (Two overnight stops are suggested for a round-the-island route. See the Squaxin Island chapter for another possible camp.)

DURATION: Full day or overnight.
RATING: Moderate. Requires a 1.5-mile open-water crossing. Currents along the route are weak.
NAVIGATION AIDS: NOAA charts 18448 or 18445 SC (both 1:80,000).
PLANNING CONSIDERATIONS: None.

Getting There and Launching

This trip originates at the Robert F. Kennedy Recreation and Education Area on the Key Peninsula. From Highway 302, turn south in Key Center onto the Gig Harbor-Longbranch Road and follow it to Home. About 1 mile south of Home, turn right on Whiteman Road (there are signs for RFK here and at the next junctions). After another mile, bear left at the fork, and then turn right a little less than 0.5 mile beyond onto Bay Road. This road turns to gravel and then forks; take the right-hand road and follow it downhill to the recreation area. Generally, there is ample parking in a lot just above the beach. Do not leave valuables in your parked car. There is also a campground nearby.

Route

For variety, follow the peninsula's shore north to a point opposite McMicken Island before crossing; on the return leg follow the Hartstene Island shore south and cross opposite RFK (this involves a slightly longer crossing). The shoreline north of RFK is pleasantly natural, with a pebble beach below high bluffs, the remains of an old pier, and a shallow lagoon with water that warms to bathtub temperatures during the summer, and, at upper tidal stages, a miniature tide race at its entrance. Hartstene Island's shore offers a similar setting. Buffingtons Lagoon, less than 1 mile south of McMicken Island on Hartstene, is another pleasant detour, though accessible only at high tide. Keep in mind that tidelands on both of these shores are private, so stay in your boat.

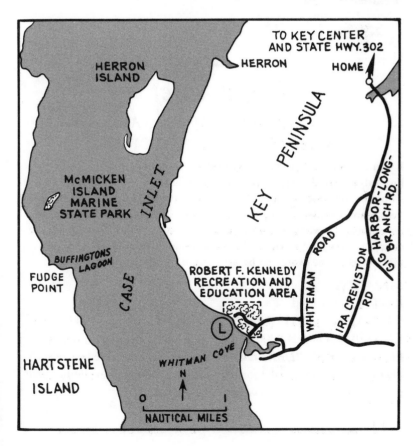

McMicken Island is particularly attractive to boaters who like the isolation afforded by low levels of development. There is no dock; a pit toilet is the only facility on shore (no water is available). Landings and access to the island are practical only on the southwest side due to the steep bluffs above the narrow beaches elsewhere. Behind this pebble and shell beach is a meadow with the handiest campsites. The fenced-in area and buildings behind the meadow are private land. A trail network circles through the dense forest north of the meadow, with occasional views out over the bluffs. Be alert for poison oak. In the forest are a few camp clearings that would be the best all-weather campsites in spite of the long haul from the beach. Fires are not allowed on the island, so bring a camp stove. The island may be closed to camping during periods of extreme fire hazard.

Carr Inlet

RAFT ISLAND, CUTTS ISLAND, AND KOPACHUCK STATE PARK

If you live south of Seattle, this is a short, easy trip, ideal for those with limited saltwater experience or for families. Distances between stopovers are not long, and there are plenty of shore attractions and beaches with warm water for wading and swimming during the summer months. The route can be altered or shortened if weather is inclement. Camping is available at Kopachuck State Park, though too distant from the water to be accessible by kayakers.

DURATION: Part day.
RATING: Protected.
NAVIGATION AIDS: NOAA charts 18445 SC or 18448 (both 1:80,000), 18474 (1:40,000); Seattle tide table (add about 30 minutes).
PLANNING CONSIDERATIONS: Consult the tide table before starting out, as low tides make for long carries to launches in the Rosedale area and may cut off access behind Raft Island.

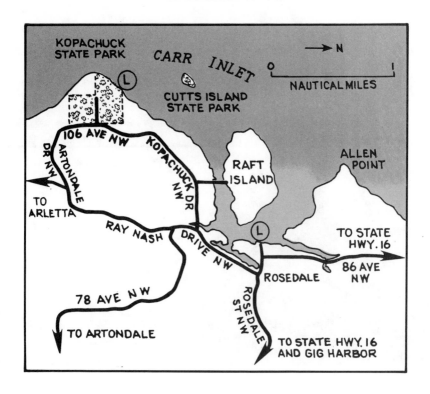

Getting There and Launching

From Highway 16 in Gig Harbor, take the Gig Harbor City Center exit (this and subsequent turns have signs for Rosedale and Kopachuck State Park). Turn left to cross over the highway, then right after 0.5 mile onto Hunt Street Northwest, and then right again onto 46th Avenue Northwest. After 1 mile, turn left at the intersection onto Rosedale Street Northwest and follow it for 2.5 miles to Rosedale.

Launching alternatives are a street-end in Rosedale, or a longer carry from parking lot to beach in Kopachuck State Park.

To launch from the street-end (Rosedale Street Northwest) in Rosedale, go straight where the road curves left at the store and gas station, passing a DEAD END sign and a playground on the right. Drive about two blocks (past a church on the left) and launch at the street's end onto a gravel beach. There is little room for more than one boat at a time to launch here at high tide when the beach is inundated. Parking is

Cutts Island

a bit limited near the street's end, so avoid blocking private residences and park farther down the street if you have more than one vehicle.

To launch from Kopachuck State Park, follow the above instructions for Rosedale, but turn left onto Ray Nash Drive Northwest and then go straight over the bridge onto Kopachuck Road Northwest after about 0.75 mile. Another 1.75 miles brings you to the park entrance. You must carry your boat approximately 0.35 mile from the parking lot to the beach. Follow a gravel service road (which is smooth enough for boat carts) to the beach.

Route

The round-trip loop from Rosedale via Raft Island, Cutts Island State Park, and Kopachuck State Park is 4 miles.

Raft Island is exclusively residential, with gorgeous homes and moored yachts well worth the rubbernecking. What looks like a good launching beach on the Raft Island Side of the bridge is not: it is restricted to use by island residents only.

Tiny Cutts Island seems larger than it really is. Steep bluffs, which increase in height toward the south end, partition the use of the island to either strolls in its madrona and fir woods above or beach hikes below. At the north end is a pebble and shell spit that extends almost to Raft Island during the lowest tides; this is steeper and easier on boats than the rockier beaches to the south. A pit toilet is located in the woods near the south end. This attractive little island cannot sustain camping or fires, and both are prohibited.

Kopachuck State Park, barely 0.5 mile from Cutts Island, brings you back to the intensity of road-accessible recreation. On a warm sunny day there are picnickers along the beach and kids splashing in the water. End the day here with a barbecue at one of the shoreside picnic sites, or perhaps a car-camping overnight in the campground at the top of the bluff.

Nisqually Delta

The Nisqually Delta is one of the finest estuaries in Puget Sound, and a good place for kayakers who like to exploit their craft's shallow water abilities and explore brackish back channels as few other boaters can. Needless to say, this is *the* prime place for birders.

DURATION: Part day.
RATING: Protected.
NAVIGATION AIDS: NOAA chart 18445 SC (1:80,000); Seattle tide table (add 30 minutes).
PLANNING CONSIDERATIONS: Most channels are negotiable at midtide or above; high tide opens up many others. A Department of Wildlife conservation license is required to use the Luhr Beach Public Access site. Nisqually Delta can be unpleasant in wind because of steep seas in the shallows and the chance of getting wet at the unprotected launch site. Waterfowl hunters are present in the State Department of Wildlife portions of the delta from mid-October to mid-January.

Getting There and Launching

From Interstate 5, take Exit 114 (Nisqually). Just south of the freeway, turn right on Martin Way and follow it for just under 1 mile to Meridian Road. Turn right here and follow it for almost 3 miles to 46th Avenue. Turn right again and go 0.25 mile to D'Milluhr Road (unsigned) to the left (a sign points to public fishing). Follow it downhill for about 0.5 mile to the parking area.

The Department of Wildlife's ramp at Luhr Beach has a moderate-size lot and a beach next to the ramp for launching. At high tide there is limited launching space on the rocky beach, which becomes sandy at lower tides and offers more space. Next to the parking area is the Audubon Society's Nature Center, which is open on selected days of the week depending on the season.

Route

Choose your own route and distance. This area is managed by the U.S. Fish and Wildlife Service and the Washington Department of Wildlife. The federal Nisqually National Wildlife Refuge includes the lower delta's tide flats and the meadows and woods of old farmland in the central portion above the dike that extends between McAllister Creek on the west and the Nisqually River on the east. State Wildlife lands include most of the lower salt marshes and most of the land along McAllister Creek.

If you arrive near high tide, you may wish to explore the myriad channels that wander across the salt marshes in the lower delta. At highest tides you may be able to pick your way through shallow channels near the dike, though a spring tide is required if you are to make it all the way across the delta by this inner route. Otherwise, head north to the lower flats to find your way to the eastern side of the delta, where you can head upstream in the Nisqually River or explore the connecting channel to Red Salmon Creek, farthest to the east. At the very northeast corner of the flats (and still within federal refuge boundaries) is a sand jetty of old pilings and a beached barge that makes a nice lunch and sunbathing stop.

If you care to venture inland, McAllister Creek at the western edge of the delta offers the possibility of many miles of small stream paddling, using the last of the flood tide to assist you on the way in and then riding the ebb back out. The creek can be paddled easily to well inland of the freeway overpass.

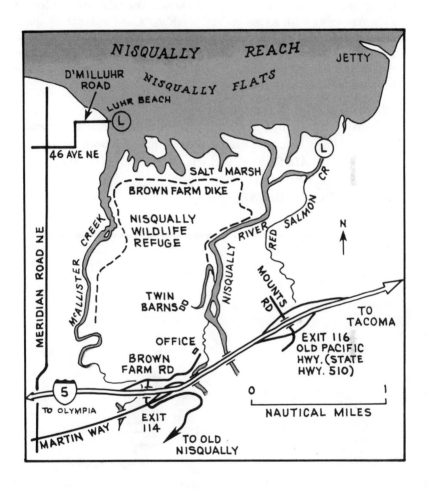

Commencement Bay

What I found here was a pleasant contrast to my expectations of a polluted industrial wasteland. Commencement Bay has a bit of everything: the wooded bluffs of Point Defiance, the "downtown" feel of City Waterway with its yachts and workboats, the melancholy quiet along the slag shores of the abandoned Asarco smelter, and the intense activity of loading and off-loading ships in one of the busiest ports in the Northwest. There is enough to fill many days of exploration in the bay and adjacent waterways.

DURATION: Part day to full day.
RATING: Protected or Moderate. The Moderate-rated Commencement Bay Loop requires crossing about 2 miles of open water.
NAVIGATION AIDS: NOAA charts 18445 SC (1:80,000), 18474 (1:40,000), or 18453 (1:15,000).
PLANNING CONSIDERATIONS: None.

City Waterway in Tacoma

Getting There and Launching

Launch sites around Commencement Bay are scattered unevenly. In downtown Tacoma, City Waterway is accessible via the floats at the city dock. Located between private marinas north of the 15th Street bridge, the waterway is marked with a sign on Dock Street. Parking may be scarce.

There are many alternatives to choose from on the shoreline between Tacoma and Point Defiance. The closest to the city is Commencement Park, located at the point that Schuster Parkway becomes Ruston Way, a little less than 2 miles from downtown. There is a good sand and gravel beach here. Similar parks are located at intervals along Ruston Way between Commencement Park and the old Asarco smelter.

In Point Defiance Park, you can set off from the launching ramp or the adjacent public floats at Point Defiance Waterfront Complex (follow Ruston Way to Pearl Street, then go right and down the hill). Or use the sand-and-gravel beach at Owen Beach. To reach it, continue into the park, past the zoo and aquarium, and drive along the bluffs to a side road that drops down to the right to the beach.

On the north side of Commencement Bay, the launch closest to the docks and industrial points of interest in the waterways is an unimproved wayside just northwest of the entrance to Hylebos Waterway on Marine View Drive. To reach it from Tacoma, take East 11th Street across the waterway industrial area about 2.5 miles to Marine View Drive, turn left, and go about 1 mile.

Farther west along the north shore of Commencement Bay is Browns Point, an appropriate launch for a loop tour of the entire bay and the closest access from north of Tacoma. From Tacoma, follow Marine View Drive west from the East 11th Street intersection for 3 miles to Le-Lou-Wa Place Northeast. Turn left and go about 0.75 mile, curving around to the right as the road becomes Tok-A-Lou Avenue Northeast. Boats must be carried about 100 yards to the gravel beach. Note that the park and lot close one hour after dark.

To reach Browns Point from the Seattle area, take Exit 143 (Federal Way) from Interstate 5. Go west on 320th Street for 4.5 miles until it intersects 47th Avenue. Go right for 0.5 mile, and then left on Dash

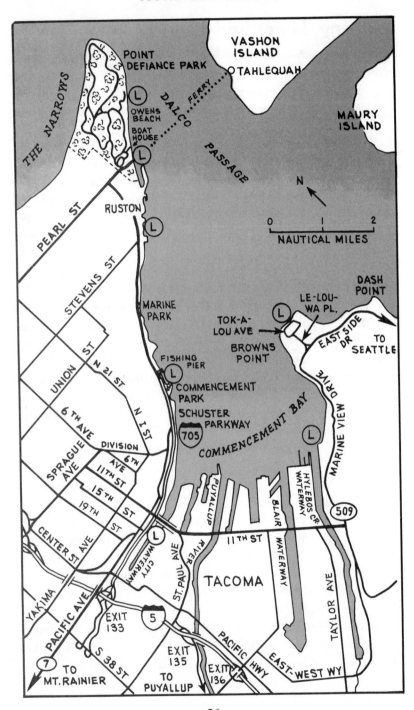

Point Road. Follow this road for 3 miles, passing Dash Point State Park—after which it becomes East Side Drive—to Le-Lou-Wa Place. Turn right and go 0.75 mile to the park.

Routes

South Shore Local Paddling: *Protected.* Choose your own distance. Pick any of the launch sites described along Ruston Way or in Point Defiance Park.

One possibility is a short trip from Owen Beach west toward Point Defiance, following the gravel beach beneath steep wooded bluffs that restrict access to the beach except for occasional trails. The current here usually flows west (strongest during the flood), and can be quite swift near the point.

Also consider paddling between Point Defiance Waterfront Complex and one of the parks along Ruston Way, perhaps in conjunction with a car shuttle. This route skirts the now-defunct Asarco smelter, beginning with its reeflike tailings of slag and cinders. This forms a steep and jumbled shoreline that I found surprisingly pleasant and interesting: seaweeds grow profusely and waves have eroded sea caves large enough to paddle into cautiously. Beyond are docks, barges, and dilapidated mill buildings, all quiet now.

A third, and more urban, alternative on Commencement Bay's south shore is the paddle from Commencement Park southeast into City Waterway, with a round-trip distance of up to 4 miles. (A much shorter exploration of the waterway can be made from the city dock, perhaps on a Sunday morning when parking is easiest to find.) You pass bulk carrier freighters being loaded as you enter the waterway and the buildings of downtown Tacoma come into view. City Waterway is the hub of recreational boating in the bay, so there are plenty of yachts to view in the many marinas along both shores. Commercial fishboats have their own floats on the northeast side of the waterway. Nearby is one of Tacoma's powerful new fireboats.

Commencement Bay Loop: *Moderate* (due to 2-mile crossing). Loop distance is about 7 miles, plus any exploration into the waterways, but can be shortened to about 5 miles by cutting across parts of the bay at any point. You can start from Commencement Park on the south shore or from Browns Point Park on the north, depending on the direction from which you approach the area. (This description begins at Browns Point.)

Begin with the crossing from Browns Point toward downtown Tacoma (or to Commencement Park if you care to make a stop there first—these are the only public facilities along the route). This course should take you past ships that usually are at anchor there. Perhaps after a look into City Waterway, start north across the old Puyallup River estuary, now among the most active maritime industrial areas in the region. There may be a fairly strong current outflow as you cross the Puyallup Waterway.

Beyond are the Blair and Hylebos waterways, where large container ships and car carriers unload. At the mouth of the Hylebos Waterway is a small military station with Army Corps of Engineers vessels. The north shore is mostly private marinas, one of which has interesting old ships positioned to form a breakwater.

Maury Island

Maury Island is connected to Vashon Island by a narrow isthmus. The most challenging route here combines the quiet charm of Quartermaster Harbor with a more arduous paddle along the "island's" south coast to produce a circumnavigation that will leave you feeling that you have seen a great deal and had a good day's exercise. For a more relaxed alternative, dabble in the harbor. If you wish to start from south Seattle, launching from Saltwater State Park involves a more demanding crossing traversing shipping lanes and possible tide rips.

DURATION: Part day or full day.

RATING: Protected, Moderate, or Exposed. The Moderate route may require committing to several miles of paddling in wind and choppy water. The Exposed area has potential tide rips and shipping traffic.

NAVIGATION AIDS: NOAA charts 18445 SC, 18448 (both 1:80,000) or 18474 (1:40,000); Seattle tide tables (add 15 minutes).

PLANNING CONSIDERATIONS: Windy weather can make the east side of Maury Island unpleasant; the shallow beaches make offshore

seas here steep and landings wet and rough. If you are going to circum-
navigate, plan for high tide to make the portage at Portage and to avoid
the extensive tideflats on the Quartermaster Harbor side.

Getting There and Launching

Maury Island routes can be reached via Vashon Island (launching at either Portage or at Burton Acres or Dockton county parks), or it can be
reached from the east shore of Puget Sound from Saltwater State Park,
which requires a 2-mile crossing.

To reach Vashon Island, take Exit 163 from Interstate 5 and follow
the West Seattle freeway. In West Seattle, this becomes Fauntleroy
Way and leads to the Fauntleroy ferry terminal. Exit the ferry at
Vashon Island and drive south to the town of Vashon. To reach Maury
Island and Quartermaster Harbor from the town of Vashon, follow
99th Avenue Southwest south about 3 miles to Southwest 225th Street,

Point Robinson

where you turn left for Maury Island. For Dockton County Park, continue past Portage on the Dockton-Portage Road about 3.5 miles. For Burton Acres County Park, continue ahead on 99th Avenue Southwest to South 240th, turn left, and then right onto Bayview Road. Both of these county parks provide parking and easy access to launches on sandy beaches.

To reach Vashon Island from Tacoma, follow Ruston Way to Pearl Street, then turn right down the hill to the Point Defiance ferry landing. Take the ferry to Tahlequah, and follow the Vashon Island Highway north to the Quartermaster Harbor area.

Portage is the popular beginning and end for island circumnavigations. There is usually parking along both of the two roads that cross this isthmus, which are connected by Southwest 222nd Street. The carrying distance between high-tide lines is approximately 200 yards. A high-tide launch or takeout on the Quartermaster Harbor side is particularly desirable, since it becomes a large mud flat at low tide. A store is open year-round and has plenty of snacks and some groceries.

To reach Saltwater State Park from Interstate 5, take Exit 149 (Kent-Des Moines). Turn left on Pacific Highway, then right onto South 240th Street, and finally right onto Marine View Drive. Follow Marine View Drive for approximately 1 mile to the entrance to the park on the right. Saltwater State Park has easy access to a sand and gravel beach, though the parking lot may fill quickly on summer weekends.

Routes

Quartermaster Harbor: *Protected*. Choose your own paddling distance. Quartermaster Harbor is a fine place for a leisurely paddle year-round; featuring warm waters and an opportunity to swim during the summer and the quiet of still, overcast days in November. The Burton Peninsula effectively breaks up the fetch, so seas are unlikely to develop extensively. Both Burton Acres and Dockton county parks are good for a picnic, though Dockton offers more shoreside seclusion with its longer beach. Tables and rest rooms are available at both.

Maury Island Circumnavigation: *Moderate*. The total paddling distance is 12 miles. The long shallow bight of Maury Island's south side is an unusual mix of wildness amid the development of the central

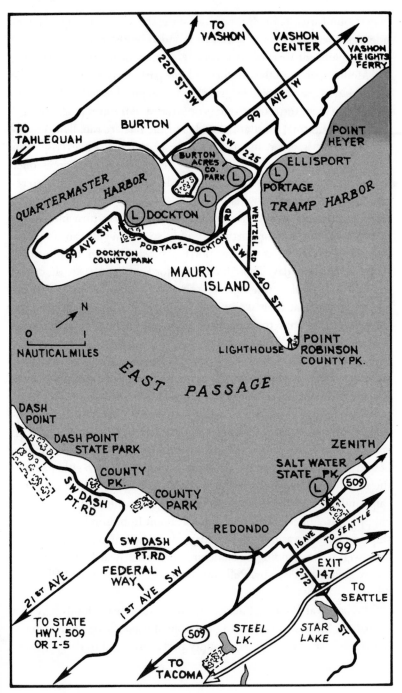

Puget Sound area. Though about half of the shoreline is occupied by residences, the remainder is grassy or wooded bluffs that invite a climb for a magnificent view of East Passage, Commencement Bay, Tacoma, and Mount Rainier in the distance. A large part of this shoreline and the bluffs behind are occupied by gravel and sand pits. I found that these do not detract from the attractiveness or interest of the area at all. Though some are operating, most are closed, and the pits are rapidly being reclaimed by grass, alder, and madrona. Rusty, derelict conveyer systems descend through the brush to rotting terminals where barges once loaded. There are no public uplands or tidelands along this shore, so respect private property rights.

The south and north shores of Maury Island can turn into rough paddling in southerly or northerly winds, so you might want to plan a circumnavigation to cover the portion most exposed to prevailing winds early in the day. Though currents for East Passage are described as weak and variable, tide rips are known to form off Point Robinson, and are perhaps at their worst when ship wakes cross them. (See the Saltwater State Park to Point Robinson route below for information and cautions about Point Robinson.)

Saltwater State Park to Point Robinson: *Exposed.* The total paddling distance is 5 miles. The crossing from Saltwater State Park, about 2 miles at the narrowest point, is easy in moderate weather. Currents in the area are listed as weak and variable, though they do accelerate around Point Robinson as water is compressed around it. Rips are possible. The primary hazard on this crossing is marine shipping bound to and from Tacoma. The traffic lanes separate to either side of the midchannel buoy; northbound ships pass to the west. Wakes from ships and the many pleasure boats that ply this channel can create quite choppy seas. I once encountered surf at Point Robinson from a passing ship's wake that was nothing less than outer Pacific Coast magnitude— look well before landing or launching, particularly at Point Robinson where ships pass close by. Pull your boat well up onto the beach when ashore.

The beach at Point Robinson and the grassy area behind the Coast Guard's lighthouse are open to the public during the day only. Up the hill northwest of the light is a county park, restricted to day use only.

Blake Island

Come to Blake Island for either a pleasant day trip or for one of the most unusual kayak-camping experiences on Washington shores. Pitch your tent, take a shower in the heated rest room, and stroll over to the longhouse for a salmon dinner followed by Indian dancing. Too civilized for you? Then choose the more primitive facilities elsewhere on this state park island.

DURATION: Full day or overnight.

RATING: Exposed, Moderate, or Protected. Tide rips may be encountered on the Moderate route; the Exposed route involves 4 miles of open water across shipping lanes, with the potential for rough seas in southerly or northerly winds.

NAVIGATION AIDS: NOAA charts 18445 SC or 18448 (both 1:80,000), and 18449 (:25,000). Seattle tide table.

PLANNING CONSIDERATIONS: Call ahead if you want a salmon dinner at Tillicum Village (see the route description for specifics).

Getting There and Launching

From Seattle, launches can be made at either Alki Point or Lincoln Park.

For Alki Point launches, take Exit 163 from Interstate 5 and follow the West Seattle freeway to the Harbor Avenue Southwest exit, then follow the road north and around Duwamish Head, where it becomes Alki Avenue Southwest. Continue to Alki Point.

To launch from Alki Point, use on of the variety of spots either north or south of Alki Point Light Station where there is access to the stony beach below the bulkheads along Alki Avenue Southwest. Find on-street parking nearby (which may be difficult to do on sunny summer weekends).

Lincoln Park has the advantage of being near the Fauntleroy ferry landing, so you can return on the ferry if necessary. Park in the south lot (note that the park closes at night), and follow the path at the park's southern boundary about 150 yards to the sand and cobble beach.

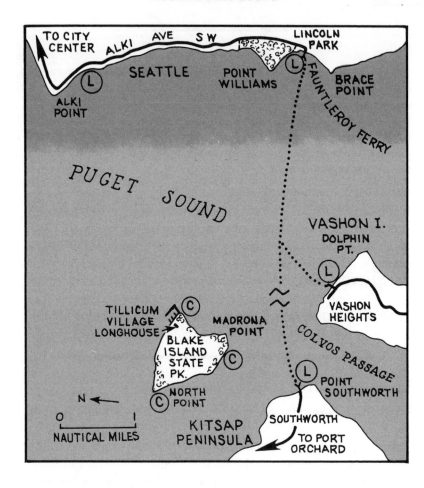

For ferry access to Vashon Island and Southworth, take the West Seattle freeway and follow the signs to the Fauntleroy ferry. To launch from Vashon Island, use the small ramp just east of the ferry dock. Parking next to the ramp is private, so unload and move cars as soon as possible to the ferry parking lot up the hill. There is no beach on either side of the ramp at higher tides, and you must be prepared to launch quickly from the ramp itself at those times without delaying other users. Do not try to get to the beach from west of the ferry dock—this is private land.

To launch from Southworth, park in the ferry parking lot just east of the dock, and follow a short path from the lot to the sandy beach.

Routes

West Seattle to Blake Island: *Exposed.* The paddling distance is over 3 miles each way across open water with heavy shipping traffic. Currents in this area usually are less than 1 knot; they are strongest on the ebb. Be prepared to use one of the alternative routes or to return to West Seattle by ferry if the weather takes a turn for the worse.

Vashon Island to Blake Island: *Moderate.* The paddling distance is approximately 1.5 miles each way, with about 1.25 miles across open water. Currents in this area rarely exceed 1 knot, but rips can occur between the two islands, particularly near the Allen Bank off Vashon Island. Colvos Passage is unique in that the current flows only on the ebb (setting north), and becomes weak and variable at other stages of the tide. Hence, this area becomes roughest on northerly winds when the ebb current opposes it.

Southworth to Blake Island: *Protected.* The paddling distance is approximately 1 mile each way, with about 0.75 mile across open water. Currents here are weak and variable as long as you stay west of Colvos Passage and head for the more westerly shore of Blake Island.

Blake Island is roughly triangular, with a paddling circumference of about 5 miles. Most of its shoreline consists of low bluffs above rocky beach, but there are sandy beaches and a shallow high-tide lagoon at the west end. Ashore, an extensive network of paths and trails interconnect.

There are three camping areas, all of which bear a camping fee year-round. On the western end of the island are sites with water (shut off during winter months) and rest rooms located up the hill. The primitive camping rate is charged for these sites. On the southern shore are two more campsites, which charge the same rate but have no water. A pit toilet is located about 100 yards east along the trail.

The eastern point (Tillicum Village) is more developed and is crowded with boaters and boat-in campers during the summer months. A breakwater encloses a boat basin with floats for the boaters who come here year-round. The campground is between the boat basin and the stony beach to the south. (If you are camping here, land on this beach unless there is a strong southerly wind and waves; in that case use the beach in the boat basin.) Most of the campsites have little or no southerly wind protection. Campsites here cost the higher full-service rate because of the heated bathrooms with coin-operated showers and other amenities.

Nearby are semi-enclosed shelters for group picnics; they also can be used for cooking and shelter during the day if not already reserved. A large central fireplace can make them cozy in cooler weather.

Western campsite, Blake Island

The most interesting element in this cluster is the Tillicum Village longhouse, featuring Indian-style baked salmon followed by demonstrations of traditional dance. The clientele is primarily people arriving by tour boat from Seattle, but boaters (kayakers included) may reserve a place for themselves by signing up at the longhouse at least one hour prior to mealtime. Service is daily during the summer and on weekends during the off-season. Call (206) 329-5700 for more information.

Eagle Harbor to Bremerton

This one of the most interesting and long-range day trips in Puget Sound, and the ability of foot passengers to carry kayaks aboard ferries allows 10 miles of one-way paddling. Leave your car in Seattle, walk your boat aboard the Winslow ferry, paddle through Rich Passage and Port Orchard to Bremerton, then take the ferry back to the city. State parks along the way make nice picnic stops with old military installations to explore. To make this into an overnight, add a 2-mile side trip to Blake Island (see the Blake Island chapter).

DURATION: Full day.

RATING: Moderate. Involves current with possible tide rips and heavy boat and shipping traffic in Rich Passage.

NAVIGATION AIDS: NOAA charts 18445 SC or 18441 (both 1:80,000), 18446 (1:25,000); Admiralty Inlet current tables corrected for Rich Passage.

PLANNING CONSIDERATIONS: Ferry schedules dictate timing here, but runs are frequent. A favorable current in Rich Passage is desirable (flood flows toward Bremerton), as it can reach 3 or 4 knots.

Getting There and Launching

Weekends are the preferred days for this trip because parking close to the ferry is easier, especially early on Sunday morning. If nothing is available under the Highway 99 viaduct across from the terminal, you may have to look some distance south along Alaskan Way.

After leaving the ferry in Winslow, turn left on the first street

Carrying kayaks aboard the ferry makes Eagle Harbor to Bremerton a feasible day trip

beyond the toll booths and look for a walkway to the left just before the apartment buildings. This leads to a small beach. Total carrying distance is about 300 yards.

At Bremerton, there is easy access to the ferry at the First Street public dock, just north of the ferry landing. Carrying distance from the floats to the ferry is about 100 yards. A tavern and a seafood restaurant are handy while you wait for the return connection.

Route

Paddling distance from Eagle Harbor to Bremerton is 10 miles. Add 4 to 6 miles for a side trip to Blake Island State Park, depending on which part you visit.

Eagle Harbor is a worthy destination in its own right, and you may want to return on another day to explore it (see Eagle Harbor chapter). But for this route, cross to the south side and out of the harbor, passing

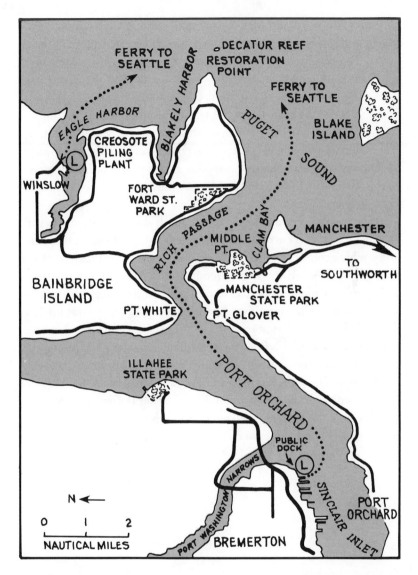

the treated-piling plant at the point. Continue alongshore to Restoration Point, being careful to stay out of the way of the ferries that run fairly close to this shore for some way before turning east toward Seattle. Off Restoration Point is Decatur Reef, a long rocky spine that can produce breaking waves or tide rips. Swing wide around the navigation marker if conditions inside of it warrant.

Both Fort Ward and Manchester state parks provide picnic tables, water, and rest rooms, as well as interesting things to explore in the vicinity. The two parks are located across Rich Passage from each other. Look for the picnic tables at Fort Ward just beyond the aquaculture pens and pier along the north shore. Old buildings from this fort, one of the first settlements in Puget Sound, are nearby and up the hill.

Manchester State Park, on the south shore west of Middle Point, also has military origins, with gun emplacements and a large brick picnic shelter that originally housed torpedos. Beach your boat at either side of this shallow bight (the center dries to a muddy foreshore). Be wary of boat and ferry wakes.

Rich Passage makes a dogleg to the south and narrows just beyond the two parks, and currents become much swifter. Keep in mind that you could encounter an incredible array of large or small vessels coming through here—even the huge aircraft carrier *Nimitz!* Currents themselves are not likely to be dangerous unless interacting with adverse winds; use them to your advantage while keeping an eye out for large vessels like the Bremerton ferry that must keep up some speed in order to stay in control in this flow. If you should encounter an opposing current, there are eddies north of Point White on the north shore and smaller ones along the south shore. The latter may be preferable since you can continue alongshore, avoiding marine traffic, into Port Orchard, where the currents weaken. Cross to the East Bremerton shore 1 mile or so beyond the eastern end of Rich Passage.

Eagle Harbor

This excursion is for kayakers who love looking at boats and enjoy seeing buildings associated with the marine industry; they're all on Seattle's doorstep, yet far from the urban bustle.

DURATION: Part day.

RATING: Protected.

NAVIGATION AIDS: NOAA charts 18445 SC (1:80,000 with 1:25,000 Eagle Harbor inset) or 18449 (1:25,000); Seattle tide table.

PLANNING CONSIDERATIONS: Higher tides allow exploration of the back bay and side coves in Eagle Harbor, which dry at lower tides.

Eagle Harbor

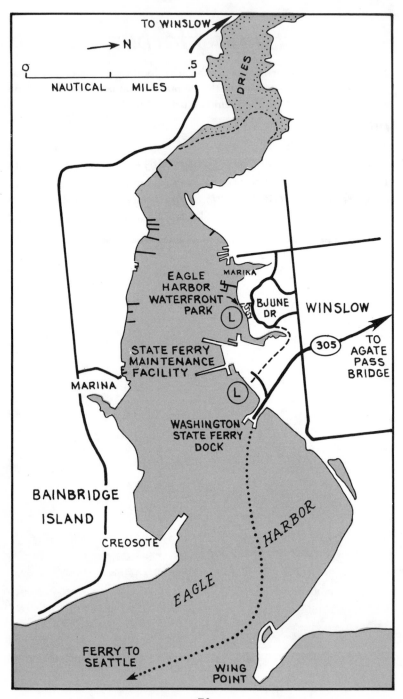

Getting There and Launching

If you are driving from the Winslow ferry dock turn left at the first traffic light onto Winslow Way (turn right if you're coming south on Highway 305) into downtown Winslow. After 0.1 mile, turn left onto Bjune Drive, and then go another 0.1 mile to Eagle Harbor Waterfront Park.

Public parking for Eagle Harbor Waterfront Park is located at the intersection of Koko Drive and Bjune Drive, as well as a short distance down Koko Drive. Launch on the gravel beach or at the boat ramp in the park.

Route

Choose your own route and distance. From Eagle Harbor Waterfront Park, there are things to see in any direction. Just east are the state ferries' maintenance facilities, where out-of-service ferries dock. Here is a chance for a close-up look at the old veterans and the superferries. Before approaching them, look carefully for activity suggesting that one of them may be about to move.

Two marinas, one directly across from the ferry docks and the other just west of the park, hold a wide assortment of fantastic yachts as well as unusual boats and barges that have been converted into live-aboards. Eagle Harbor also is popular with boaters (some of them live-aboards) who prefer to anchor out. Their craft are concentrated in the middle third of the harbor, and include floathouses on barges or rafts, old tugs and fishing boats, and yachts.

Along shore are active industries (including a plant that produces treated pilings at the harbor entrance) and many relics from the past—sheds and warehouses on pilings, some abandoned and some still in use. A tiny, shallow cove across from the ferry dock is particularly picturesque for its shoreline structures as well as its seclusion.

The very back of the harbor is less developed and less popular with boats because it dries on lowest tides, but it is worth exploring if the tide is in. Midway back is an old warehouse dock that is a remnant of the berry-farming industry that once thrived in the vicinity.

West Point, Shilshole Bay, and Golden Gardens

This area, west of Seattle's Ballard neighborhood, is a good place for both cautious sea outings for new kayakers, and more lengthy and challenging routes for the more experienced. It includes popular and secluded sunbathing beaches, more yachts than anywhere else in Puget Sound, and sunset views of the Olympic Mountains. At present, the Lake Washington steelhead run at the locks in Salmon Bay produces the highest density of sea lions in Puget Sound. The West Point area's beaches are lightly used (requiring a walk to reach them), and are backed by the woods and bluffs of Seattle's largest natural reserve, Discovery Park. The West Point route could be extended into Elliott Bay to connect with the launch points and routes described in the Elliott Bay chapter, perhaps with a car shuttle.

DURATION: Part day or full day.
RATING: Protected or Moderate. The Moderate route may require committing to a distance of rough paddling to return to the launch site.
NAVIGATION AIDS: NOAA charts 18445 SC (1:80,000), 18446 (1:25,000), or 18447 SC (1:10,000); Seattle tide table.
PLANNING CONSIDERATIONS: Lower tides offer more beaches (many are backed by rock riprap that makes unsuitable landing places at high tide).

Getting There and Launching

Launch sites are limited to either Golden Gardens Park at the north end of Shilshole Marina or Commodore Park in Magnolia, just below the Chittenden Locks. There is no car access to beaches in Discovery Park (West Point). To reach Golden Gardens Park, take Exit 172 (85th Street) from Interstate 5 and go west on 85th Street for about 3 miles. Where it ends turn right on Golden Gardens Drive Northwest and wind down the bluffs to the beach area.

At Golden Gardens, use the parking lots just behind the beach or if they are full, park along Seaview Avenue Northwest. Launch at the beach or at the ramp just inside the marina breakwater to the south. The parking lots are closed at twilight.

Commodore Park is reached by following Commodore Way west from Fishermen's Terminal on the south side of the ship canal. Launch at the beach just east of the railroad bridge. Take Exit 169 (45th Street)

Sea lions hauled out on buoy, Shilshole Bay

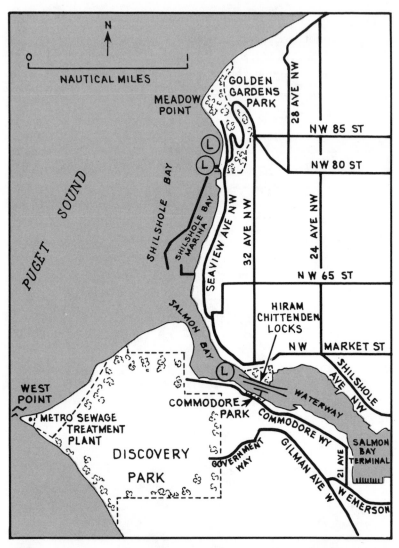

from Interstate 5 and go west on 45th Street. After 1 mile, bear right where this becomes North 46th Street and later when it becomes Northwest Market Street. After descending the hill, follow Northwest Market Street to 15th Avenue Northwest. Go left and follow it south for 1 mile. Just after crossing the Ballard Bridge, go right on Emerson Street. After passing Fishermen's Terminal, turn right on West Commodore Way and follow it past the Chittenden Locks to the park.

A 5-mile shuttle between these points could be worthwhile. From Commodore Park, follow Commodore Way and then West Emerson Street to 15th Avenue Northwest, and cross the Ballard Bridge. Go left on Northwest Market Street, and follow it to Seaview Avenue Northwest, and go north to Golden Gardens.

Routes

Golden Gardens to Salmon Bay via Shilshole Marina: *Protected.* Choose your own paddling distance; the one-way trip beween Golden Gardens and Commodore Park is about 2 miles. Novice paddlers may prefer to stay in the bay just off Golden Gardens beach, which gets some protection from both northerly and southerly seas. Or explore inside the marina, being especially watchful for traffic entering and exiting at the breakwater entrance. Landings to use the rest rooms or restaurant at Shilshole can be made at the dock closest to the parking lots behind the gas docks.

An outflowing current is always present in Salmon Bay due to the drainage from the Lake Washington Ship Canal. Most of it can be avoided by using eddies close inshore, particularly in the shallows on the south side. Boat traffic may be very heavy in this area, so alongshore routes are the safest for kayakers. Pleasure craft waiting for the locks may be numerous just below the railroad bridge.

At this writing, sea lions are very active between the launching beach at Commodore Park and the dam. Stay close to shore when approaching or leaving the park and do not paddle closer to the dam.

Golden Gardens to West Point: *Moderate.* The round-trip distance is 4 to 5 miles. Keep in mind that there is no car access to the West Point area, committing you to return to Shilshole Bay in whatever conditions develop. Tide rips are possible off West Point, and the bar there can produce breakers some distance from the point. Be especially watchful for ships' wakes here and when landing elsewhere along the route.

Popular landing spots are at the gravel and cobble beach just north of the rock riprap at the sewage plant and at West Point itself; choose whichever side is sheltered from the wind. Rest rooms are located about 0.25 mile up the road from the point. For more seclusion, continue about 1 mile past the point and into the bight below the bluffs, beyond where most beach walkers from West Point usually venture. The foreshore here is very flat, so you will likely have to carry your boat some distance if spending time ashore. Watch for the many boulders scattered throughout this intertidal area.

If you follow the route within the marina on the way out, consider a straight course back across the bay toward Golden Gardens from West Point if conditions are conducive. Sea lions sometimes haul out on the buoys here (keep your distance). At midtide, a sandy beach appears on the outside of the marina breakwater, providing the most secluded stop in this area, as it is not accessible by land.

Port Madison and Agate Passage

The northern shore of Bainbridge Island and the adjacent Kitsap Peninsula make an easy "impulse" paddle for local dwellers, and are easily accessed from Seattle by ferry and car too. Though the area's shores are primarily residential, with an emphasis on ritzy homes, there also are two state parks and an Indian museum along the winding course of a narrow inlet and the fast waters of Agate Passage. Possibilities for short or longer paddles, perhaps with a car shuttle, are numerous.

DURATION: Part day.
RATING: Protected or Moderate +. The Moderate + route involves crossing Agate Passage in current up to 3 knots with possible heavy pleasure boat traffic.
NAVIGATION AIDS: NOAA chart 18446 (1:25,000) or 18445 SC (1:80,000); Admiralty Inlet current tables with corrections for Agate Passage.
PLANNING CONSIDERATIONS: Strong wind, particularly from the south, can make a wet launch or landing on the beach at Fay Bainbridge State Park. Agate Passage currents are the only significant ones in this area, but they are strong enough to be worth planning around.

Getting There and Launching

Launch choices are Fay Bainbridge State Park on the northeast corner of the island or, for the Agate Passage area, the Suquamish Museum, Old Man House State Park, or Suquamish Center. The car shuttle distance between Bainbridge Park and the Agate Passage launch sites is about 8 miles.

To reach Bainbridge Park, turn north from Highway 305 about midway between Winslow and the Agate Passage bridge on East Day Road (watch for signs to Fay Bainbridge State Park). After 1.5 miles, go left onto Sunrise Drive Northeast. Go another 1.7 miles and turn right into the park. Rest rooms, drinking water, and picnic facilites are provided.

Launching at Bainbridge Park is from a gravel beach facing east onto Puget Sound. A slight bulge in the shoreline offers some protection

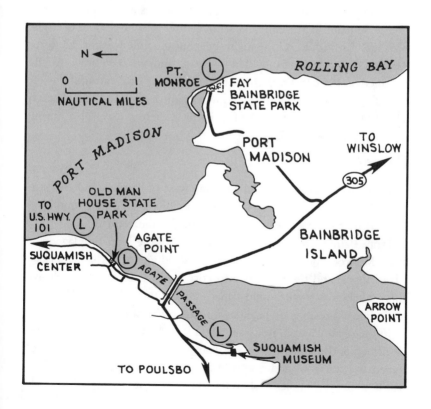

from northerly wind waves, but the launch is exposed to waves from the south and to ship wakes.

For either Old Man House State Park or Suquamish Center, turn north from Highway 305 about 0.25 mile west of the Agate Passage bridge on Suquamish Way. Old Man House Park is 1.35 miles down this road at Division Avenue. Turn right there and go another 0.35 mile.

This small state park has limited parking, a vault toilet, drinking water, and picnic facilities. Interpretive displays describe Indian dwellings that were located here, including Chief Sealth's. A sand beach for launching is located about 100 yards from the parking area.

For Suquamish Center, continue another 0.35 mile along Suquamish Way and turn right where the road makes a dogleg to the left as it enters this small town. Park in the small lot and launch next to the boat ramp on a gravel and cobble beach (cars can be driven to the water's edge briefly to unload). Cafes and grocery stores are located nearby.

The Suquamish Museum and Tribal Center is located south of Highway 305. Turn south off the highway about 0.5 mile west of the Agate Passage bridge onto Sandy Hook Road, and go 0.35 mile to the entrance on the left. From the parking lot, carry boats around the left side of the museum building and down a path leading to a gravel beach (about 50 yards carrying distance). Facilities here are available during the museum's open hours.

Routes

You can choose between local paddling west of Bainbridge Park or at Agate Passage, or connecting the two areas for a 5- to 7-mile round trip (or half that distance using a car shuttle for the return).

From Bainbridge Park, you might explore the high-tide lagoon at Point Monroe (the entrance is on the west side, close to the Bainbridge Island shore) and then paddle into Port Madison to see the exclusive shoreside homes there (round-trip distance is about 4 miles). There are no public shorelands or facilities on this route after the park.

In the Agate Passage area, you might launch at any of the three sites described and paddle locally, or arrange a shuttle (road distance between the museum and Suquamish Center is about 2.5 miles) and paddle along the 3 miles of shoreline through Agate Passage. The sandy beach and picnic facility at Old Man House State Park make a nice stop along the way. From the water look for the park on the west shore between the inshore navigation marker and the "2" buoy at the north end of Agate Passage.

Currents in Agate Passage can attain almost 4 knots under the highway bridge, but are rarely as much as 2 knots in the northern portion (cross between Agate Point and Old Man House State Park if the currents are strong and unfavorable). A current flowing against either a north or south wind could make dangerous seas here, and the combination of strong currents, eddies around the highway bridge abutments, and heavy pleasure-boat traffic could give less experienced kayakers problems. Most difficulties and hazards can be minimized by paddling as close to the beach as possible, though the currents there could still be strong enough to make slow progress against them in the area under the highway bridge.

Lake Union

If you are an experienced Seattle paddler, chances are you have already explored Lake Union, as the majority of resident paddlers probably took their first strokes here. Lake Union has perhaps the highest year-round density of sea kayaks, perhaps nation- or even worldwide! It is usually smoother than local saltwater destinations and the water is warmer than the Sound in the summer months, making it a good place to develop skills. And the fascinating shoreline of shipyards, houseboats, yachts, and shore-accessible eateries and shops makes it a repeat destination for any Seattleite with a few hours to spare. A tour of Lake Union could be combined with excursions either east or west along the ship canal, perhaps with a shuttle to launch points in Ballard or the Arboretum.

DURATION: Part day.
RATING: Protected.
NAVIGATION AIDS: NOAA chart 18447 SC (1:10,000). A Seattle street map is probably as useful.
PLANNING CONSIDERATIONS: Go anytime.

Getting There and Launching

There are at least six public shoreline areas suited for launching and two sea-kayak renters within boat-carrying distance of the lake. Some parking is available near all of them (street curb in some cases), but may be difficult to find on nice summer weekends.

For the south, west, or east shores of Lake Union, take Exit 167 (Mercer Street) from Interstate 5. Take the first right onto Fairview Avenue North and go one block to the lakeshore. (The Chandler's Cove complex is at this location.) Continue straight for the east shore, or bear

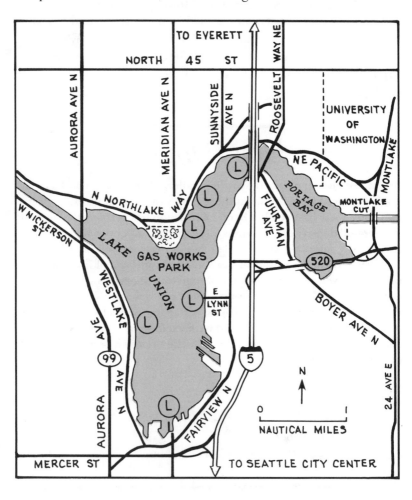

left onto Valley Street for the west shore (bearing right after about three blocks onto Westlake Avenue North).

For the north shore of Lake Union, take Exit 169 (45th Street) from Interstate 5. Go west on 45th Street 1 mile to Stone Way North. Turn left and follow Stone Way almost another mile to the lakeshore. Go left on Northlake Way for Gas Works Park and other launch sites along the north shore.

NORTH END OF LAKE UNION

Boat ramp off Northlake Way at the foot of Sunnyside Avenue North: Park along the bike trail.

Gas Works Park: Park in the park's lot or along Northeast Northlake Way at the park's eastern boundary. The closest beach is at the eastern edge of the park, a 100-yard carry from the lot. The Swallows' Nest, a retailer that rents sea kayaks, is about one block up Meridian Avenue North from the east edge of Gas Works Park.

WEST SIDE OF LAKE UNION

There is no public access along Westlake Avenue North. The Northwest Outdoor Center rents kayaks at the water's edge at 2100 Westlake Avenue North (look for the standing kayak and for a sailboard shop just north).

EAST SIDE OF LAKE UNION

South Passage Point Park: At the foot of Fuhrman Avenue, below the freeway bridge. Parking may be scarce. Beaches are rocky except for a small gravel beach centered under the freeway bridge.

East Lynn Street Minipark: A small beach at the foot of East Lynn Street. Parking on side streets may be difficult.

Chandler's Cove Development: At the junction of Fairview Avenue North and Valley Street, just east of a Burger King. Some public parking is nearby; be sure not to use that reserved for local businesses. Use the gravel beach just below the lawn.

Routes

The lake is slightly less than 2 miles in length and about 4.5 miles around if you follow the shores between the freeway bridge and the

Fremont Bridge. All shores have restaurants with dock access, ranging from burgers to seafood to gourmet dining. The north shore has Gas Works Park, shipyards, and plenty of yachts to view. The west side is primarily yacht moorage. The Lake Union houseboat community comprises much of the east shore, along with NOAA's research-ship facility and a shipyard. The south end has a seaplane base, the Naval Reserve Center, the historic lumber schooner *Wawona,* and the Center for Wooden Boats, where all manner of small wooden craft can be rented. Just west is the Chandler's Cove area, a good place to go ashore (use the beach) to purchase a snack or window-shop.

Lake Union's moods change with the pulse of the city. Try it on a fair summer's evening, when the myriad sails of the Duck Dodge race frame the sunset, or on a calm Sunday morning in winter, when both city and water are quiet and you will meet few others besides hardy kayakers like yourself. On a stormy day, Lake Union is a good practice place for experienced paddlers who want to work on their wind-paddling technique in a reasonably safe setting.

Duwamish Waterway

Among shipyards, barge landings, ship hulks, the roar of factories and foundations of long-gone activities is Kellogg Island—a remnant of the original meandering Duwamish River and the last natural shoreline in the Elliott Bay area. Though a portion of the island was covered with dredging spoils, vegetation now grows thickly and herons, cormorants, and other waterfowl abound. The Port of Seattle will likely keep the island in its natural state and has an ongoing program to develop a number of nearby shore access points and mini-parks in the lower Duwamish Waterway. Pick your own route here depending on your interests, or combine one with the nearby trips described in the Elliott Bay chapter, especially Harbor Island.

DURATION: Part day.

RATING: Protected. However, ship and barge traffic is heavy in this confined waterway, and new kayakers should ensure that they have sufficient boat control to stay out of the way before venturing into the waterway, especially during the ebb current times.

NAVIGATION AIDS: NOAA chart 18450 (1:10,000) or 18445 SC (1:80,000, see 1:40,000 inset); Seattle tide table.

PLANNING CONSIDERATIONS: A strong ebb current (the flood current is negligible) can make upstream travel harder, and may pose problems for new kayakers around pilings or when avoiding ship or barge traffic. Consequently, you may wish to avoid these currents during periods of falling tide. At low tide, shores are quite muddy.

Getting There and Launching

There are six launch points in the lower Duwamish area, on both sides of the waterway. Different sites could be used with a shuttle, making possible a linear paddle through the entire lower Duwamish beginning at the First Avenue Bridge (number 6) and ending at the Alaskan Way Public Access (number 3), for example. I've listed these in order of preference.

1. End of Diagonal Street: This is the closest access for visiting Kellogg Island, directly across the waterway. Follow Highway 99 to about 0.25 mile south of the Spokane Street overpass and turn west on Diagonal Street (if northbound, turn at the next light after the hedges on the left of Federal Center South; if southbound, turn at the second light after the overpass). Follow this street about three blocks to its end at the waterway. Public access and parking are to the left and center of a tiny bay. At this writing, development of a barge dock for the adjoining cement plant with an adjacent park and launching for portable boats is planned in this area.

2. East Waterway Junction: Located beneath the West Seattle freeway bridge across from Harbor Island, at the junction of the East and Duwamish waterways. Coming from West Seattle, take the old Spokane Street drawbridge across the Duwamish, cross Harbor Island, and turn right immediately after crossing the East Waterway bridge. Westbound traffic must follow Spokane Street onto Harbor Island, make a U-turn, and recross the East Waterway bridge to reach the launch. There is parking and a gravel ramp that makes launching easy at any tide.

3. Alaskan Way Public Access: This access allows launching near the middle of the East Waterway, and is also a launch point for exploration of Harbor Island and Elliott Bay. Located about 0.65 mile south of the Coast Guard facility, it is at the point where Alaskan Way South becomes East Marginal Way South. Look for gray fuel storage tanks and a sign for East Waterway Viewpoint. Access to the water is down rock riprap, but this is likely to be improved in the future.

4. Terminal 105 Viewpoint: Located off West Marginal Way Southwest less than 0.25 mile south of the West Seattle freeway interchange, and just north of Southwest Dakota Street. This park includes parking and a picnic shelter, but no rest rooms. Those launching boats are asked to use the access point at the south end of this facility (follow the gravel trail). Be careful of shipping traffic that cuts very close to the north end of the park and a barge operation just to the north. Access to the water is down rock riprap that has been graded to some extent and will likely be improved further.

5. Terminal 115 Viewpoint: Another minipark, located off West Marginal Way Southwest just north of the First Avenue bridge. Turn east on Southwest Michigan Street and follow it to the parking area at the end. No facilities. Access to the water is down rock riprap. Future improvement is likely.

6. First Avenue Bridge Boat Launch: Located just east of the First Avenue bridge, off South River Street, this concrete ramp may be crowded during the warmer months or the salmon season, when it is the base for Indian gillnetters. Limited parking is nearby.

Routes

Choose your own route in the waterway; there are shipyards, barge loading docks, cement plants, derelict ships, and much more. About halfway between Diagonal Street and the First Avenue bridge are the "emerald mines"—shoreline on the east side where a glass factory has dumped beads of melted glass.

Be sure to include Kellogg Island and the channel west of it. The island is close to the west side of the waterway, across from and slightly south of the Diagonal Street launch point. Just to the north are derelict ships. Kellogg Island was originally much larger Anderson Island, and here was the approximate northern edge of the Duwamish estuary before the filling of Harbor Island and the south Seattle industrial area began. The waterway was dredged to the east of the original channel

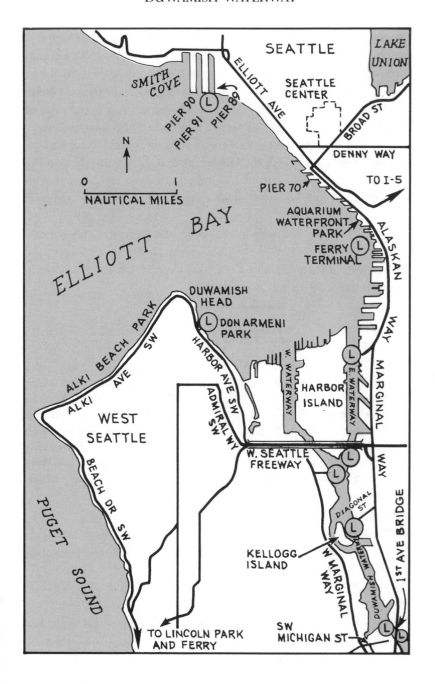

bend, creating the island, and its original height at just about high tide was increased by dredging spoils dumped on the south end. This miniature wilderness of brambles, brush, and hidden grassy glens might be worth a gingerly stroll on a sunny spring day (look for the sole white birch lost among the alders). Late in the summer, a cornucopia of largely unpicked blackberries make a fully sufficient reason for a visit.

The shore on the west side of the old channel bend behind Kellogg Island is also a park, with the Duwamish bike path quite close to the shore here. Steep banks make it an impractical launching spot, though you could certainly scramble up for a picnic at the top. There are no facilities at this writing.

The old channel course behind Kellogg Island may dry on low tides. Though the ebb current in the Duwamish can run up to 1 knot, the flow in the old channel is slight and makes a good way to get upstream, riding back down in the main channel.

Elliott Bay

This is one of my favorites. Shipyards with naval frigates or an Alaska ferry in drydock intrigue me, and I never tire of my routes deep under the waterfront's piers. The routine also calls for a stop along Alaskan Way for fish and chips. Your interests may not match mine, but you are sure to find plenty if you like seaport cities. A longer outing could be made by exploring south around Harbor Island or in the Duwamish Waterway (see the Duwamish chapter), or around Magnolia and West Point to Shilshole Bay (see the West Point, Shilshole Bay, and Golden Gardens chapter).

DURATION: Part day.

RATING: Moderate. Ship and ferry traffic is heavy, landings are not allowed along much of the waterfront, and the circle route involves crossing 2 miles of open water and busy traffic.

NAVIGATION AIDS: NOAA chart 18450 (1:10,000) or 18445 SC (1:80,000, see 1:40,000 inset); Seattle tide table.

PLANNING CONSIDERATIONS: High tide is more pleasant, but some riprap shores have small low-tide beaches where landings are not possible at higher tides.

Getting There and Launching

There are four launch sites spaced around Elliott Bay.

In the Magnolia-Interbay area, use the bank next to the parking area at the north end of Elliott Bay Park, adjacent to Pier 90. Turn west from Elliott Avenue West (just south of where it becomes 15th Avenue West) onto West Galer Street, and follow it around to the left as it becomes 16th Avenue West. Step over the low railing next to the lot and launch on the cobble and mud bank (may be very muddy at low tide).

In downtown Seattle, launch at the public docks at the foot of Washington Street. Parking nearby may not be easy; look for a spot to the south along Alaskan Way.

Ferry in Harbor Island drydock

Farther south, along Harbor Island, use the Alaskan Way Public Access, located at the Point where Alaskan Way South becomes Marginal Way South. See the Duwamish Waterway chapter for details.

On the west side of Elliott Bay, launch at Don Armeni Park on Harbor Avenue Southwest. From the West Seattle freeway, take the Harbor Avenue exit and drive north about 1 mile to the park. Use the launching ramp, as there is little beach. Rest rooms are provided.

Route

Paddle locally from any of the launch points, or make a circle tour of as much of the bay as desired. I usually launch at Don Armeni Park, and then paddle straight across Elliott Bay toward Pier 70 or a point farther south. Then I follow the waterfront south and take a break at the Washington Street floats (perhaps sending one member of the party north along Alaskan Way for fish and chips). Beyond is the container terminal (Pier 46), which has a cavernous space beneath with plenty of room to paddle between the cement footings. This seemingly endless straight tunnel is one of the more unusual sea kayaking experiences I have had.

A note of caution about paddling under any piers: technically you are trespassing on leased tidelands and doing so at your own risk. Because of safety and liability concerns, the Port of Seattle cannot condone this use and could prohibit it at any time. Use common sense. Be sure that there is plenty of headroom, look for wires that could be live, and avoid nearby ships (avoid the ferry dock entirely) and container loading operations. *Never* paddle between a ship and the dock.

At the Harbor Island shipyards, you must stay at least 100 feet to seaward. That is still plenty close enough to ogle the drydocked ships with propellers, bo1w thrusters, and sonar domes exposed for all to see.

Playing in seven-knot current, Deception Pass

North Puget Sound

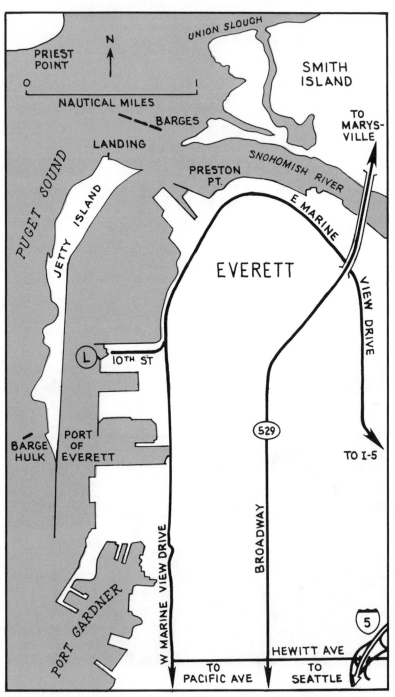

Everett Harbor

JETTY ISLAND AND VICINITY

Just beyond the mills and marinas of Everett's waterfront, Jetty Island has both wildness and antiquity—seabirds and sea lions can be seen near the rotting barges that were beached long ago to stabilize the shifting sandbars of the Snohomish River estuary. This is the closest opportunity for a solitary beach hike in the Seattle area (guaranteed in the winter months). At this writing, construction is under way on the Navy's homeport facility on the east side of the Snohomish River channel south of the marina, to be completed in 1992. This will not affect Jetty Island nor access in the Snohomish channel. The city of Everett does plan some recreational enhancements for the island.

DURATION: Part day.

RATING: Protected.

NAVIGATION AIDS: NOAA charts 18423 SC, 18441 (both 1:80,000), 18443 (1:40,000) or 18444 (1:10,000); Seattle tide table.

PLANNING CONSIDERATIONS: Extensive tide flats make avoiding the lower tides essential. The highest tides give you access to small lagoons and backwaters on Jetty Island and make circumnavigation of the island shorter. Currents in the Snohomish River channels can be strong on both the ebb and flood tides.

Getting There and Launching

From northbound Interstate 5, take Exit 193 (Pacific Avenue). Turn left under the freeway, and go about five blocks to Broadway Avenue. Turn right, and drive two blocks to Hewitt Avenue. Turn left and follow Hewitt through downtown Everett and downhill toward the waterfront. About three blocks short of the mill buildings on the shore ahead, turn right onto Marine View Drive. Follow this street for almost 2 miles, bearing left at the Y and railroad overpass, and passing the marina on the left. Turn left onto 10th Street for the public launch ramp and marine park. Use the launch ramps and docks or, if they are very busy, the shoreline on either side. Note the closing hours for the park and be sure to return before then.

Route

The Jetty Island circumnavigation is approximately 4 miles. Shorter excursions to northern Jetty Island and the vicinity are attractive in themselves. For the circumnavigation, plan the direction in accordance with the Snohomish River channel flow direction, which is stronger than that on the west side of Jetty Island (the narration sequence here assumes a counterclockwise direction of travel).

From the launching ramp, follow the main Snohomish River channel upstream, passing extensive log storage facilities on the right. Across the channel is Jetty Island. Its shore here is used for log storage too, but less actively. At high tide you may be able to find routes behind the logs along the island's shore, winding through shallow passageways among the rotting pilings and derelict, forgotten logs. Eventually, the water opens up to the left as you round the north end of Jetty Island.

The elevations of seabed and land barely differ in this river outwash area. Jetty Island itself is hardly more than a long sandbar covered with salt grass, Scotch broom, and an occasional tree. Over the years, wooden barges have been beached to control the movement of sand and silt. Walk inland toward the navigation marker tower at the north end of the island and you will find the old timbers and iron drift pins and bolts of barges that were beached and burned here long ago and are now completely surrounded by land.

Better-preserved barges are located about 0.5 mile north of Jetty Island. They are beached in a line that extends, along with countless pilings, most of the way across to Tulalip's shore to the north. If you appreciate wooden ships, the barges are worth the visit for a close look. These oceangoing vessels have all the workmanship that shipwrights of that era put into the more memorable sailing ships—diagonal triple planking, huge scarph joints, wooden treenail fastenings, and massive one-piece timbers no longer obtainable at any price.

The western edge of Jetty Island is an unbroken beach, with shallow waters warmed enough by the summer sun for a swim at high tide. At low tide, it becomes a sandy tide flat a mile or more wide. More hulks of old barges are found here and there along the beach.

A large colony of sea lions resides in this area during the late winter and spring (usually between February and May). At lower tides they

Winter fog along Jetty Island

move offshore, often floating in large somnambulant clusters. When the tide is in they like the beached barges or even the logs behind Jetty Island in the Snohomish River channel. Beware—they have little fear of humans and are apt to make threatening gestures to kayakers. (Many paddlers feel sea lions are potentially the most dangerous of all the marine mammals.)

The southern end of the island narrows to become a stone jetty for the last 0.5 mile. As currents may be strong against you for the paddle back upstream in the Snohomish River to the launching ramp, you may want to shorten the loop by portaging across the island north of the stone jetty—a distance of 100 yards or less, depending on tides and logs stored on the east side.

Once in the river channel, you have the choice of following the wilder island shoreline or crossing to inspect the marina's fishing boats and yachts. There are a variety of shops here with groceries, food, and spiritous beverages.

Skagit River Delta

The Skagit River Delta is a birder's paradise and more. A maze of marshland channels, river dwellers' shanties and floathouses, and even overgrown pre-World War II coast artillery emplacements are included in the rich estuary country within the Skagit Wildlife Area.

DURATION: Part or full day.

RATING: Protected.

NAVIGATION AIDS: NOAA chart 18423 SC (1:80,000) or USGS 7.5 Minute Series (1:24,000) topographic map for the Utsalady Quadrangle; Seattle tide table (add about 20 minutes).

PLANNING CONSIDERATIONS: Midtide or higher (at least 4 feet above mean low water) is required for paddling outside the main Skagit River channel and outside Swinomish Channel. Both Skagit River and Swinomish Channel reverse their currents with the tide (at least one hour after the tide change for the former; Swinomish Channel is not easily predicted). Currents affect paddling efforts to and from all launch locations.

You may wish to avoid the heavy bird-hunting period from mid-September through December; contact the Department of Wildlife for specifics. Each member of your group must have a state Department of Wildlife conservation license in his or her possession to go ashore in Skagit Wildlife Area. These can be purchased at stores that sell fishing and hunting licenses.

Getting There and Launching

Choose from launch sites along the Skagit River or in downtown La Conner. An approximately 10-mile car shuttle could be made between them.

From Interstate 5 take the La Conner-Conway exit and branch right to Conway soon after. Continue about 5 miles on Fir Island Road. For the lower river launch at Blake's Skagit Resort and Marina, turn left on Rawlins Road. Located approximately 1 river mile above the delta area, Blake's is the lowest launch point on the North Fork of the Skagit River. The resort charges a launch fee, which also covers parking.

A Department of Wildlife launch site is located farther upriver. Turn right off the highway onto Moore Road about 0.35 mile beyond Rawlins Road, just before the North Fork bridge, then take the first unsigned dirt road to the left 0.25 mile beyond at the S-curve. Department of Wildlife conservation licenses are required to use this launch site.

To launch from La Conner follow the above directions on Fir Island Road, which changes to Chilberg Road, and continue 5 miles beyond the North Fork bridge to La Conner. The La Conner public boat ramp is located below and just north of the Rainbow Bridge. After entering La Conner, turn left on Maple, then right on Caledonia Street, left on

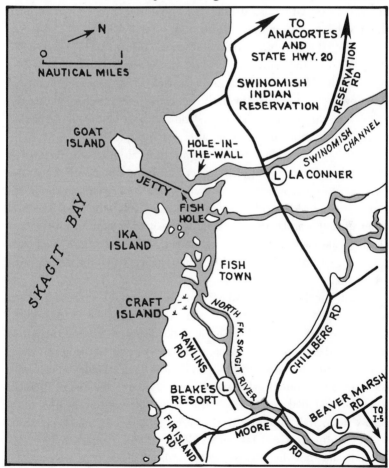

Third, and finally right on Sherman Street. The ramp is straight ahead at the waterfront. There is a fee for the use of the ramp. Park in the lot across the street or along the street beyond.

Routes

Skagit River to Craft Island: *Protected*. The paddling distance is 3 to 5 miles each way. Time your start to ensure that you will have mid- to high tide in the delta once you get downriver. The distance to the shallow delta area from Blake's is about 1.5 miles, and about 3 miles from the upper river launch. There is a downstream current from both river launch sites during the ebb, and an upstream flow as far as the upper launch on larger flood tides (except during heavy river runoff), though this begins as much as an hour after low tide.

Heading downriver approximately 1 mile below Blake's, you reach a sharp bend to the right; just beyond are pastoral farm buildings and river dwellers' houses and shacks on the right bank—the community of Fish Town. Just downstream on the left is the first side channel into the delta. Take this channel for Craft Island and keep bearing left (the distance is little more than 1 mile after leaving the river).

Craft Island is really a hill jutting up from an otherwise flat marsh and tidelands to the west of the river as it nears the mouth. From the top you can see a sweeping panorama of the marshlands to the north and south and, at low tide, the vast gray tide flats to the west. This and other upland islands are a particularly sensitive habitat for raptors, including bald eagles and red-tailed hawks. If you go ashore, avoid approaching or disturbing these birds, particularly when the nesting sites are in use.

Timing for the Craft Island excursion is important, as the side channel to it is dry below midtide. If you have the time, you may wish to head downriver at early ebb, paddle to the island, and spend the last of the ebb and early flood lunching, exploring, or just enjoying the view.

If your tide timing was off for paddling to Craft Island, you can walk there after returning to the launch point. Drive to the end of Rawlins Road beyond Blake's. A rough trail accessible on lower tides leads across the marsh meadows to the island (about 0.75 mile each way).

La Conner to Goat Island to Skagit Delta: *Protected*. The paddling distance for the loop is 7 miles; additional side trips are possible.

Most of this loop can be paddled at tide heights of 3 feet or more. (Avoiding low tide is not as critical here as for the Craft Island route.) However, at the lower end of the tide you would be scooping sand much of the way in a foot or less of water; getting out to wade and tow your boat may prove easier in spots. Spending the low-tide interval exploring Goat Island would be worthwhile if you can afford the time.

From the public launch at La Conner, follow the channel south through the twisting narrows of Hole-in-the-Wall. Beyond, the channel opens to flats with intertidal islets and shallow waterways that invite exploration if the tide is in. To the south is a log storage area bounded by a stone jetty extending to Goat Island. The route later returns through a tiny gap in this jetty.

Goat Island has both the dense forest and the grassy meadows with

Coast artillery emplacements on Goat Island

madrona trees that are typical of the more arid San Juan Islands. On the northwest end is Fort Whitman, a component of the extensive coast artillery defenses for Puget Sound built at the turn of the century. There are mounts for three guns in the emplacements, with associated rooms and tunnels similar to those found at Fort Warden and Fort Casey state parks. Such defenses were obsolete by World War II, when aircraft became more effective than coast artillery against invading fleets. Most of Goat Island was ceded to the state a few years after the war.

To reach the emplacements, look for the old dock along the island's north shore. Behind it is a rocky, muddy beach and the start of a rough trail that climbs to the right. Follow this about 250 yards to the battery.

As with other islands in the Skagit Wildlife Area, this is a particularly sensitive habitat for resident raptors. The Department of Wildlife asks that you respect the privacy of these birds, particularly during spring nesting. As elsewhere within the Skagit Wildlife Area, no camping is allowed.

Paddling around the south side of Goat Island brings you into the shallowest part of this route, though enough water can be found in the shifting channels of the Skagit River on all but the lowest tides. On ebb tides and the first portion of floods, downstream currents will make moving up into the delta hard and slow work, with few eddies to take advantage of.

At this point, you could take time to explore the many sloughs off the Skagit River's channel and perhaps even cut through the delta to Craft Island, about 2 miles to the east, if the tide is high enough.

The return to Swinomish Channel from the Skagit River is via the "fish hole" in the jetty—a small opening allowing migrating salmon that made a wrong turn into Swinomish Channel to get back to the river. Located about 200 yards from the eastern end of the jetty, this gap is not visible as you approach from upriver, but follow the jetty and you will find it. The hole is dry below midtide.

Skagit Island, looking toward Deception Pass

Hope and Skagit Islands

Though currents are swift in this area, the protection of nearby Fidalgo and Whidbey islands makes Hope and Skagit reasonable destinations when other places are a bit on the rough side. Ashore on these state park islands are grassy hillsides with flowers in season, forest trails, campsites, and plenty of sand and gravel beaches for sunbathing.

DURATION: Part day to overnight.

RATING: Moderate +. Currents can produce turbulence in certain areas and rough seas when opposing southerly winds. Avoid strongest currents at the west end of Hope Island unless you have the skills to handle strong eddy lines and tide rips.

NAVIGATION AIDS: NOAA charts 18423 SC, 18421 (both 1:80,000), or 18427 (1:25,000); current tables for Deception Pass.
PLANNING CONSIDERATIONS: Currents here are dependent on those in Deception Pass. The flood flows south. If possible, plan to catch the flood current going to the islands and the ebb for the return.

Getting There and Launching

Launch from the Cornet Bay area of Deception Pass State Park. Follow signs to Cornet Bay from Highway 525 about 1 mile south of the bridge and go about 1.25 miles to the launching ramp area. Use the gravel

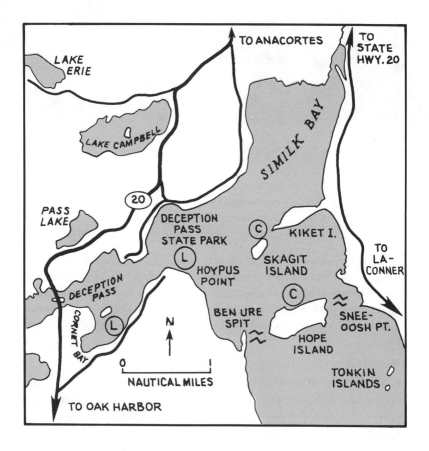

beach just below a timbered bulkhead in front of the parking area or, if the tide is high and covers the beach, use the launching ramp or floats. For overnight parking, use the lot across the road from the boat launch.

For day trips, you could continue 1 mile past Cornet Bay boat launch to the end of the road at Hoypus Point (the old ferry landing before the bridge over the pass). Launching here cuts at least 1 mile from the one-way distance. Overnight parking is not allowed here; use the overnight lot at Cornet Bay.

Route

From Cornet Bay to Hoypus Point, the state of the current dictates how far offshore to paddle—head out 100 feet or so to catch a ride on the flood current. If it is ebbing, there are eddies that make easy paddling along the tree-lined gravel beach to Hoypus Point, but you will have to fight the brunt of the current as you round the point. Likewise, there are some eddies south of the point toward Ben Ure Spit that will help against an ebb.

You may wish to cross directly from Hoypus Point to Skagit Island, adjusting to offset the effects of the current as you go across. Its strength diminishes during the second half of this 1-mile crossing.

Skagit Island is rocky and steep along its north and western shores. There are gravel and shell beaches at the east and southeast ends, and a primitive campsite at the east end. An unenclosed pit toilet is located in the woods behind the site. A trail circles the island, winding through fir and salal forest on the north side. The south side of the island is a series of rocky meadows interspersed with madronas, with lots of nice spots for lunch in the sun.

Hope Island is far larger. There are five campsites in a very shallow bay on the north side, with a pit toilet but no water. Trails circle this island, but most visitors prefer hiking the beaches or paddling alongshore to walking in the thick forest. Gravel beaches on the south side of Hope Island are the biggest attraction for day-use paddling, with chances for walking and secluded rest stops.

Currents at both the east and west ends of Hope Island are swift and dangerous for anyone not skilled in dealing with moving water. If you are unsure, avoid going around to the south side, or go around and back via the east end, where currents are a little weaker. Both ends can have sharp eddy lines and possible tide rips. Stay close inshore on the east end, where you will probably need to cross only one eddy line, and then paddle in eddies the rest of the way around.

The west shore has a very strong eddy line that has capsized kayaks in the past. The current between Hope Island and Ben Ure Spit (about 0.35 mile distant) may be as swift as you can paddle, requiring hard work to get across against an opposing flow without losing too much ground. The flow along the spit is slower, but still takes hard paddling upstream against a flood current to reach the eddies north of the spit.

Deception Pass

Deception Pass offers outstanding beauty that can be explored safely on the fringes of the high-current area in the pass itself. You can also paddle through the pass when currents are weakest (beginners should avoid the pass unless certain of correctly identifying the slack current time; there is plenty of easy paddling in areas of little current yet still within view of Deception Pass's full magnificence).

Experienced paddlers eager to expand their skills can expend some adrenaline practicing in Washington's strongest currents—crossing eddy lines, developing bracing reflexes in swirls and turbulence, and maybe descending into a whirlpool! Currents mostly average 5 or 6 knots at their maximum (the occasional strongest ones exceed 8 knots) in the pass. Speeds rapidly decrease within 0.5 mile of both sides of the pass.

Routes in Deception Pass can be combined with those in the Hope and Skagit Island area to the east (see the Hope and Skagit Islands chapter).

DURATION: Part day.

RATING: Protected, Moderate +, or Exposed. Heavy boat traffic in the pass may create rough conditions.

NAVIGATION AIDS: NOAA charts 18427 (1:25,000) or 18423 SC (see 1:25,000 inset for Deception Pass); Deception Pass current tables.

PLANNING CONSIDERATIONS: Seek or avoid strong current periods depending on your skills and preferences, using the Deception Pass current tables. Launch and takeout locations depend on current flows, described below. The flood current flows east through the pass. Avoid times of strong wind from the west, particularly during ebb currents, which can produce particularly nasty seas and tide rips.

Getting There and Launching

There are three launch sites within Deception Pass State Park. Which you use depends on where you wish to paddle and the state of the current in the pass. (Tactics for planning with currents are described under routes.)

Bowman Bay is accessed from Highway 525 about 0.5 mile north of the Deception Pass Bridge. This is a good start for protected paddling north of the pass or for one end of a shuttle trip (about 3 miles driving distance) through the pass to Cornet Bay. Launch on the gravel beach in front of the parking lot.

West Beach is the easiest access to the pass from the west. Turn off Highway 525 about 0.5 mile south of the bridge and follow signs to the West Beach parking lot. In windy weather or when a large swell is penetrating the Strait of Juan de Fuca, the sand and gravel West Beach can have substantial surf. If it is not to your liking, a 200-yard-long path leads from the parking lot to a protected launch on North Beach just behind West Point.

Cornet Bay serves paddling to the east of the pass. Follow signs to Cornet Bay from Highway 525 about 1 mile south of the bridge and go about 1.25 miles to the launching ramp area. Use the gravel beach just below a timbered bulkhead in front of the parking area or, if the tide is high and covers the beach, use the launching ramp or floats.

Routes

Bowman Bay: *Protected.* Paddling anywhere within this bay, located between Rosario Head and Reservation Head, will avoid dangers from currents, and waters should be relatively smooth. There are plenty of rocky shorelines to explore, plus opportunities for lolling on the beaches or exploring ashore at Sharpe Cove to the west or at the spit adjacent to Lottie Bay to the east. Portaging across to Lottie Bay is easy, and Lottie Bay is rated Protected to its mouth, where currents can be strong.

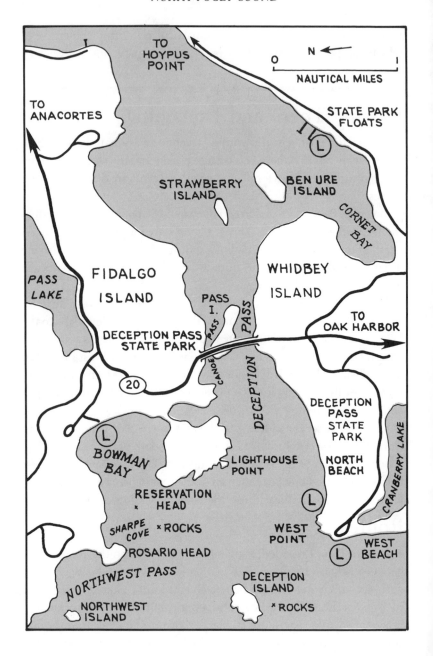

West Area Exploration: *Moderate +* . Currents west of Lottie Bay generally are less than half the strength of those predicted for the pass, and probably are suitable for intermediate paddlers with some experience with currents. If there is any doubt about the abilities of members of your party to handle currents, avoid times when the currents in the pass are predicted to exceed 5 knots. Crossing the mouth of the pass from Bowman Bay to North Beach should be done cautiously during flood currents that could set you toward the stronger currents in the pass. This area can be extremely rough when swells from the Strait of Juan de Fuca oppose an ebb current flowing out of the pass. At such times or in windy weather, the eastern portion of the pass area (Cornet Bay) is a more prudent choice.

Plan to spend some time exploring the rocky shores between Reservation Head and Lottie Bay, where you will find a number of pocket beaches for secluded lunch stops (ashore, this area is accessed by a trail from Bowman Bay). In one of these coves, a steel ladder leads from sea level to the heights of Lighthouse Point, which provides an excellent vantage into Deception Pass.

The park extends north to include part of Rosario Bay and also Northwest Island and Deception Island. Neither of these islands is developed and access is not easy. Gravel beaches on the north side of Deception Island offer fairly easy landings on lower tides but it's a hard scramble to gain access to the island above.

Cornet Bay: *Protected.* Explore this bay as far north as Ben Ure Island (private) or west toward Hoypus Point, about 1 mile from the boat launch. Currents in Cornet Bay are weak and often flow the opposite direction as in the pass, forming a long, tapering back eddy on ebbs along the shore toward Hoypus Point. At the latter, currents may be strong, and accompanying rips make it unsuited for Protected-rated paddling. Likewise, the strong currents and eddies around Strawberry Island are appropriate only for experienced paddlers.

Bowman Bay to Cornet Bay (or Reverse) through Deception Pass: *Moderate +* . You can see it all in this 3-mile traverse through Deception Pass. Timing for at least near-slack in the pass is critical; you may want to arrange your travel to catch the last of the current going your way at the beginning or the new current at the end. Allow plenty of time to explore the coves west of the pass. Stops ashore near the pass are easy on the beaches at Gun Point and another small beach directly north across the channel. Pass Island has fair access ashore on rocks on the east end. Access at Strawberry Island is similar.

Boat traffic in the pass is a significant hazard, especially if the current forces boats to speed up or reduces their control. Canoe Pass, the smaller passage to the north of Pass Island, is the safer and more interesting way through when currents are weak, as little traffic goes this way. However, a bend in this channel reduces visibility for oncoming powerboats.

Deception Pass Current Play: *Exposed.* Depending on the current strength and on your skills, capsizing here is probable (a wet- or dry suit is advisable) and you should be prepared to rescue members of your party if it should happen. A number of Seattle-area sea-kayak retailers and outfitters hold classes for intermediate-level paddlers in Deception Pass to give them practice in negotiating currents and bracing. They usually seek current strengths of about 5 knots and may have an outboard-powered inflatable standing by. Five knots offers eddy lines strong enough to capsize the kayaker who does not prepare for them, especially in narrower boats. Seven knots requires strong leaning and bracing in all boats when crossing eddy lines, and can create swirl zones and boils that may be intimidating to all but the most blasé whitewater boater. On ebbs, whirlpools form downstream from Pass Island but do not last. On strong floods, more persistent whirlpools form on the edge of the main channel east of Pass Island. These are a thrill for those who care to chase them down and put one end of their boat down in the vortex.

Canoe Pass is preferred to the main channel for eddy play, primarily because of the boat traffic going through the pass at all but the strongest current times. Wakes can make big breakers as they meet eddy lines on either side of the channel. On ebbs Canoe Pass has eddies on both sides just west of the bridge, and ferrying back and forth from one to the other is easy. On floods a series of small eddies forms close to the island's steep rock face, and a long back eddy forms along the opposite shore. Hopping from one to the other is possible, but requires more maneuverability than during ebbs. Watch out for sharp barnacles along both shores that can make capsizing there perilous.

Looking east from Point Doughty at Orcas Island's northern shore

San Juan
Islands
Area

Burrows Island

The paddling at Burrows Island is interesting and exhilarating—sheer rock and lively currents. Ashore you will find an abandoned Coast Guard light station that is now a state park. Hike beyond the station to steep grassy shorelines or climb the hill above for a spectacular view of southern Rosario Strait.

DURATION: Part day.

RATING: Moderate. Currents can exceed 2 knots and tide rips are likely. Wind can make this area quite dangerous during times of strong current.

NAVIGATION AIDS: NOAA charts 18423 SC or 18421 (both 1:80,000) or 18427 (1:25,000); Rosario Strait current tables with corrections for the Burrows Island-Fidalgo Head area.

PLANNING CONSIDERATIONS: Use the flood current to travel west in the channels on either the north or south side of Burrows Island and for rounding Fidalgo Head from the south. Flood currents here are generally stronger than the ebbs.

Getting There and Launching

Choices for launching are either Skyline Marina, the closest to Burrows Island, or Washington Park, which adds another mile or so of paddling around Fidalgo Head. These two launch points are about a 0.5-mile walk apart, so consider starting at Washington Park and taking out at Skyline Marina.

From Anacortes, follow signs for the San Juan Island ferry, about 4 miles west of town. Continue straight where the ferry traffic curves right down the hill to the ferry landing. After 0.5 mile, turn left for Skyline Marina and go another 0.5 mile. Take Hughes Lane to the right and park along the south side of the street near the end. Launch at the sand beach just a few yards' carry from the circle at the end of the road.

For Washington Park, continue straight past Skyline Way and go right at the Y intersection. Park in the "A" lot (note day-use restrictions) and carry your boat across the lawn to the gravel beach.

Route

Most of the shoreline of Fidalgo Head, Burrows Island, and neighboring Allan Island is steep rock, with grass and madronas growing above, steep drop-offs that allow close-in paddling. Beaches are infrequent. All of Fidalgo Head west of Skyline Marina is in Washington Park; expect to see lots of people along its shores. Public land on Burrows Island is restricted to the 40 acres and 1,000 feet of shoreline in Burrows Island Light Station State Park on the island's west and southwest corner. Visitors ashore here are rare. There are no public lands or tidelands on Allan Island.

Expect to find strong eddy lines and nearby tide rips in the channels separating Burrows Island from Fidalgo Head and Allan Island. It is possible to ferry across these currents to reach the island, though you may have to work hard to maintain your position as you cross.

The only landing at the park on Burrows Island is on a gravel beach just north of the light station. The challenge here is scaling the steep

Rosario Strait from Burrows Island Light Station

rocks on the north side to the old supply-landing facility, which can be precarious in wet weather. Above are the equipment shed and residence building, boarded up since the station was automated. The lighthouse and a horn (which operates in all weather) are located at the point.

To the south are wild and rugged grassy slopes above cliffs that drop

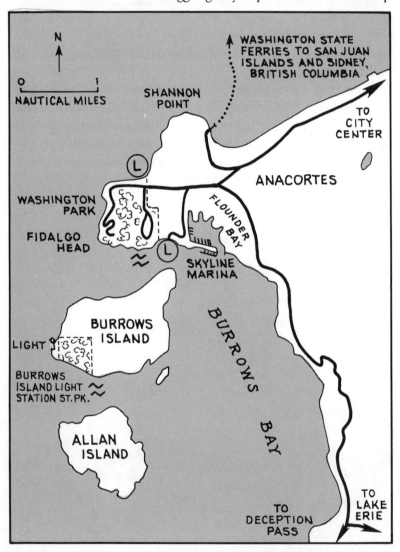

to the water, a chance for exploring where few others go. If you would like a vantage point, follow this shore a few hundred yards around to the east and climb up the rocks and grassy slopes to the hilltop. To get there from the light station, walk behind the lighthouse into the trees (the shoreline here is not negotiable). A path was being cleared here in 1989. Beyond, the trees and brush thin out enough to pick your own route. Be wary of steep drop-offs to the cliffs below. This is no place for small children.

Padilla Bay

One of a handful of national estuarine sanctuaries, Padilla Bay is a vital rest and feeding stop for migratory waterfowl (particularly black brant) and a nursery for countless intertidal creatures. Due to the mixture of fresh water from its sloughs and salt water from the bay, its tidal marsh habitat hosts a rich diversity of plants and animals. At low tide, Padilla Bay's mud flats extend for miles, so timing for high tide is essential to explore its tidal marshes and sloughs. For a better under-standing of what to see here, stop at the sanctuary's Breazeale Inter-pretive Center just north of Bayview State Park.

DURATION: Part day.

RATING: Protected. The hazard is low here in the sense that waters are rarely too deep to stand in. However, winds in this area can be strong and seas in the shallows steep.

NAVIGATION AIDS: NOAA charts 18423 SC, 18421 (both 1:80,000), or 18427 (1:25,000); Port Townsend tide table (add 30 minues for high tide time and one hour and 15 minutes for low tide time).

PLANNING CONSIDERATIONS: High tide (at least 5 feet) is essential here to explore these huge tide flats and adjacent sloughs. A falling tide could leave you stranded with a mile or more of soft mud between you and the water. This area is often windier than the surrounding area. Most of the bay is open to bird hunting from mid-October to January.

Getting There and Launching

Launch at either Bayview State Park on the bay's east side, Indian Slough (southeast side), the Swinomish Channel boat launch (southwest side), or March Point (west side).

From Interstate 5, take the Anacortes (Highway 20) exit and go west 16 miles to Bayview-Edison Road, opposite the Farmhouse Restaurant. Go north on this road for Indian Slough or Bayview State Park. The road crosses the slough after about 1 mile; park at the trailhead for the Padilla Bay Shore Trail just beyond it. At Bayview State Park, turn right into the park and then take the underpass down to the picnic area. Launch at the sand beach. The sanctuary's Breazeale Interpretive Center is located about 0.5 mile farther north along the highway. It is open 10:00 A.M. to 5:00 P.M. Wednesdays through Sundays, all year.

For the Swinomish Channel boat launch, continue west on Highway 20 another 1.5 miles and turn right just before the bridge. The turnoff to March Point is 0.25 mile west of the Swinomish Channel bridge. For more details about March Point, see the Saddlebag Island chapter.

Route

Though the entire bay makes for interesting and scenic paddling, there are some portions that you should avoid. The Department of Wildlife has identified two areas where wintering brants are vulnerable to disturbance. One area extends north from Bayview State Park almost to Joe Leary Slough. Confine paddling to south of the park. The second area is just north of the railroad bridge in Swinomish Channel and east along the dike for about 0.5 mile. Give the tidelands in this area a wide berth if you launch from the boat ramp in the channel, and paddle on east to explore the areas in and around Telegraph and Indian sloughs. Or, go west from the channel to find more salt marshes and sandy spits resulting from dredging the channel.

There are no public shorelands other than the launching points in the estuary sanctuary, and at this writing most of the tidelands are still in private ownership pending litigation. Two good routes would be from Swinomish Channel to either Bayview State Park or March Point, using the facilities ashore there (minimal at March Point). Both involve about 6-mile round trips, or more if you explore the sloughs on the way to the state park.

Saddlebag Island

So named because it is almost two islands with a connecting isthmus, Saddlebag Island has both meadow and forest for walking in, and primitive campsites in the low area between. The short paddling distance makes it suitable for a last-minute camping decision. It can be combined with further exploration of nearby Padilla Bay.

DURATION: Part day to overnight.

RATING: Moderate. Requires crossing open water where tide rips are possible.

NAVIGATION AIDS: NOAA charts 18421 or 18423 SC (both 1:80,000), or 18427 (1:25,000); Port Townsend tide table (add one hour).

PLANNING CONSIDERATIONS: Though all tides are fine for the Saddlebag Island route, lower tides add some carrying distance at the March Point launch and restrict access to other parts of Padilla Bay.

Getting There and Launching

The easiest and closest launch is from the end of March Point, site of the conspicuous refineries visible to the north of Highway 20 a few miles east of Anacortes. Turn north off Highway 20 just west of the twin Swinomish Channel bridges onto the March Point road. After about 0.75 mile, bear right across the railroad tracks. Continue about 2.5 miles farther to the end of the point. Launch anywhere between the boat ramp and the oil tanker pier underpass. Public access to these gravel beaches is by the grace of Shell Oil Company. Many recreational vehicles park here during the warmer months.

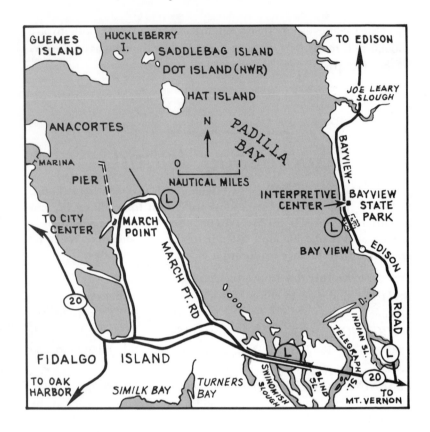

Route

The one-way distance from March Point to Saddlebag Island is 2 miles. Currents along this route are slight until the vicinity of Hat Island, where an east-flowing flood or west-flowing ebb current may be encountered. Tide rips may occur in this area. Hat Island makes a nice first landfall along the route, though you should not land on this privately owned island. Its steep rocky sides make interesting alongshore paddling. Dot Island, located just southeast of Saddlebag Island, is a wildlife refuge, so stay 200 yards offshore from it. Eagles are often seen in its trees.

Good landings on Saddlebag Island are found at both the north and south beach at the center of the island, or at a more secluded pocket beach on the west side (with a steep climb to the meadows above).

Saddlebag Island, with Dot Island on the right

Campsites are scattered throughout the isthmus area. There are pit toilets, but no water. The most secluded sites are above the low bluff facing the south beach. Those near the north beach are the most accessible from the water, and are the most protected from southerlies during the off-season. As is typical with most islands in this area, the south side has rocky meadows on both its east and west hills, accessed by informal trails. The north side is more wooded.

Cypress Island

The wild ruggedness of Cypress Island, the chance for a hike to catch the panoramic views from Eagle Cliff, and the three public camping areas almost evenly spaced around the island contribute to its popularity with kayakers. And, unique in the San Juan Islands, ferry trips are not required. In 1989, the Department of Natural Resources purchased the majority of the island, and now owns about four-fifths of it, which is managed for recreation.

DURATION: Overnight or two nights.

RATING: Moderate + .

NAVIGATION AIDS: NOAA charts 18423 SC or 18421 (both 1:80,000), 18430 (1:25,000); Rosario Strait current tables (with corrections for Bellingham Channel, Strawberry Island, Guemes Channel, or Shannon Point, depending on your location) or the Canadian *Current Atlas.*

PLANNING CONSIDERATIONS: This is one of the most popular routes in the San Juan Islands, and campsites may not be available on weekends at Pelican Beach—the kayaker's favorite—during the peak season. Strong currents can create very dangerous localized conditions off Cypress Head in Bellingham Channel; avoid big tides or aim for slack current in this area. Currents strongly affect traveling speeds on all sides of the island; generally, use floods for going north and ebbs for the return.

Getting There and Launching

You can choose between launch sites at the Guemes Island ferry landing on Guemes Channel just west of Anacortes, or at Washington Park, a city park about 1 mile west of the San Juan Islands ferry terminal. As detailed below, the currents dictate paddling schedules from each of these launch sites to and from Cypress Island.

To reach the Guemes Island ferry landing in Anacortes, drive north through town and then left as indicated for the San Juan Islands ferry. Go about 0.25 mile and then turn right on I Street. Go straight ahead and downhill to the Guemes Island ferry terminal. Park in the unpaved

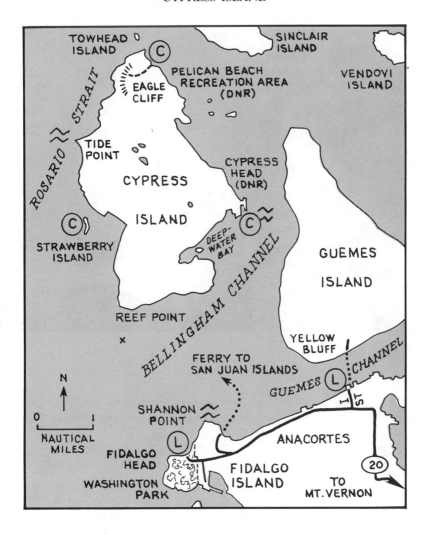

lot just west of the ferry lot, and launch on the sand and rock beach (at this writing, the area is scheduled for development as a park).

To reach Washington Park in Anacortes, follow the signs through town to the San Juan Islands ferry terminal, about 4 miles past Anacortes. At the top of the hill above the ferry terminal continue straight at the Y where ferry traffic bears right, and go another 0.5 mile to Washington Park. Overnight parking is allowed in the lot at the Y behind the park entrance sign. To get closest to the beach, drive down

Pelican Beach

to the day-use parking area to unload, and then move your car to the overnight lot. At present there is no charge for overnight parking, but it is probable in the future.

Route

A complete circumnavigation of Cypress Island is approximately 15 miles. Use the Canadian *Current Atlas* to visualize and plan your trip around the currents in Bellingham and Guemes channels and in Rosario Strait. The stage of the tide affects which launch point is the more practical for starting out at that time.

The launch point at the Guemes Island ferry landing is probably safer and more versatile for starts at different tide stages than the Washington Park put-in near Fidalgo Head. Currents sweep strongly around this body of land, and the crossing from there to Cypress Island is more than 2 miles. As the ebb current sets southwest, reaching Cypress Island from the Fidalgo Head/Shannon Point area on even average tides can be almost impossible. There is a good possibility of being swept out into Rosario Strait in the process. This situation also would be very rough with a southerly wind.

On strong ebb currents, the Guemes Island ferry launch offers a safer and easier option. Cross the 0.5-mile-wide Guemes Channel (usually possible on most tide stages), and then work west along Guemes Island and up its western shore. Wait until the current slacks before crossing Bellingham Channel to Cypress Island.

On flood currents, Washington Park may be an easier launch point, as the current flowing northward can be ridden into Bellingham Channel. From the Guemes Island ferry landing, you will have to fight the east-flowing flood current (though it generally is weaker than the ebb) in Guemes Channel until rounding the corner into Bellingham Channel.

Midway up Bellingham Channel is Cypress Head. This protuberance creates back eddies, strong eddy lines, and associated rips that can be very dangerous, particularly on large ebbs. In May, 1984, a stable double kayak capsized in this turbulence, and the paddlers were lucky to be rescued after a considerable time in the water (see *Sea Kayaker* magazine, Summer/Fall 1984). If you approach while the current is flowing, hug the shoreline. The back eddy extends 100 feet off Cypress Head, and the safest route is right along the shore inside the kelp.

Cypress Head is a DNR Recreation Site with campsites in the woods on the head and at the neck connecting it to the main island—a great place to watch the action in a big ebb exchange. Landings are at the rock and gravel beaches on both the north and south sides of the neck. (You will also find a dock and float on the north side during the warmer months.) The three campsites on the west end of the neck are the most convenient from the beaches, but the more distant sites in the woods offer better weather protection. There are the usual pit toilets, but water is not available.

About 0.5 mile east of the northern end of Cypress Island is Pelican Beach, another DNR area, developed with help from the Pelican Fleet (owners of a type of beachable cruising sailboat often found hauled up on this fine pebble beach). One of the nicest features here is Eagle Cliff, a spectacular 840-foot overlook of the entire Rosario Strait area, and very popular with campers who climb up for the sunsets. The trail is a little more than 1 mile long. The climb is easy except for the last few hundred yards. The open-meadowed uplands around Eagle Cliff invite independent exploration (be careful of the sheer drops), and there is an alternative loop to another overlook.

At the beach there is camping space for about four groups, and though more can be accommodated, the narrow beach strip quickly becomes crowded (mostly with kayakers). Behind is a covered picnic shelter and pit toilets (water is not available).

The currents along the Rosario Strait side of Cypress Island are strong enough to merit planning around them, though there are enough eddies in this irregular shoreline to work against them for most of the distance. Topography is at its most impressive here; Eagle Cliff and other precipices are far above.

Strawberry Island is yet another DNR recreation area that provides simple campsites along the southwest side of this 0.25-mile-long island. Access is via a small beach at the south end, which is gravel at high tide but rocky at low water. As elsewhere along Rosario Strait, be wary of huge breaking wakes from passing tankers when you beach your boat.

Camps are up to 100 yards north; those with the best weather protection are the most distant. A trail continues north up the island to an overlook. Water is not provided.

From Reef Point at Cypress Island's southern end, formulate tactics for crossing to Fidalgo Island (if that is your destination) with the powerful offshore currents in mind. On a flood tide, crossing to the Washington Park area can be exhausting or even impossible. Ebbs, however, make this easy (barring southerly winds), with some course correction to counteract westerly drift. If you are bound for Guemes Channel, use a slack or early flood current to cross to Yellow Bluff on Guemes Island and then get a lift from the flood up Guemes Channel to the ferry landing. In calm weather, this crossing to Guemes Channel can be made directly and quickly from Reef Point with the right timing: use the last of the ebb to cross toward Washington Park, and position yourself to catch the southerly portion of the new flood current that will sweep into Guemes Channel, rather than north up Bellingham Channel.

Lummi Island

Though it has most of the amenities of the San Juan Islands, Lummi Island is sufficiently off the beaten cruising path to be missed by most boaters. The southern end has all the ruggedness that makes alongshore paddling so interesting, and a campground to match. This trip could be extended to Clark Island, covered in a separate chapter, which has an alternative route via Lummi Island.

DURATION: Overnight.
RATING: Exposed or Moderate. The Moderate route involves currents and some open-water paddling in a channel that can become very rough with southerly winds. The Exposed route involves more of the same with potential commitment to miles of paddling in rough conditions.
NAVIGATION AIDS: NOAA charts 18423 SC, 18421 (both 1:80,000) or 18424 (1:40,000); Rosario Strait current tables or Canadian *Current Atlas*.
PLANNING CONSIDERATIONS: Moderate currents in Hale Passage affect paddling ease along these shores. Strong currents along Lummi Island's southwest shores can be hazardous against a contrary wind.

Getting There and Launching

Launch from Gooseberry Point in the Lummi Indian Reservation. From Interstate 5, take Exit 260 (Lummi Island-Slater Road), and turn west onto Slater Road. After almost 4 miles, turn left onto Haxton Way. Follow Haxton Way for 6.5 miles to the Lummi Island ferry landing at Gooseberry Point.

Parking and access to the beach at Gooseberry Point have been in contest at various times, as this is within the Lummi Indian Reservation; ask in the store next to the ferry landing. Parking is probably most appropriate in the lot south of the ferry dock, in an out-of-the-way spot so as not to conflict with ferry parking. Launch from the sandy beach next to the dock.

Routes

Hale Passage Loop: *Moderate.* The total paddling distance is about 13 miles. This pleasant overnight trip follows Lummi Island's east shore south to a campsite at one of the more interesting DNR recreation sites. Return can be by the same route or, for a little variation and weather permitting, across Hale Passage to Portage Island for the return to Gooseberry Point.

Although the crossing from Gooseberry Point to Lummi Point is only about .65 mile, swift currents of up to 2 knots can make paddling to the opposite shore exhausting, and it can be dangerous in winds opposing the current. Hence, time this crossing for near the slack, and then catch the ebb down Lummi Island's shore if possible. Though the alongshore currents are not terribly swift, they are persistent (few eddies) and tiring against a contrary tide.

Northern Lummi Island is a mixture of farms and residences. There is little wild shoreline on the northeastern side. Along Hale Passage, homes become sparser as you come abreast of Portage Island on the opposite shore. They gradually diminish as the shoreline steepens and disappear altogether just north of Inati Bay, where there is also a large gravel pit. Round that last point, and you will find that Lummi Island is wild to the south.

Inati Bay is a fine spot for a stretch onshore, though it is likely boats will be moored there during the cruising season. The Bellingham Yacht Club leases the head of the bay for a boaters' shore stop and has installed pit toilets and fire rings. The woods behind are well worth a walk inland, and there is an old road that eventually leads to the main road from the north.

Lummi Island Recreation Site is less than 1 mile south of Inati Bay, beyond gradually steepening rocky shores. This DNR site is a particularly interesting one, as it is fitted into the rocky benches of a steep hillside. Steps and switchbacking trails connect two tiny coves to upland campsites that make use of every level spot. The result is a charming campsite especially attractive to kayakers because it provides poor moorage for other boats with no protection against southerly blows. The campsites are more secluded than those at other such recreation areas, making this a nice place to stay even if others are present. As with other DNR sites, there is no water service, but garbage cans and pit toi-

Two of the three coves, Lummi Island Recreation Site

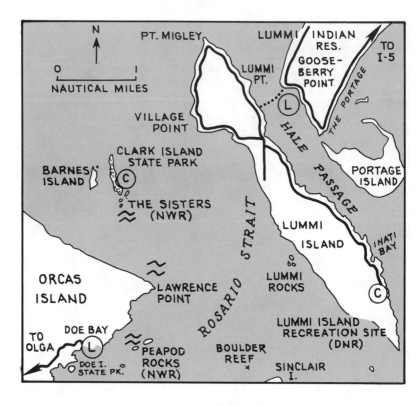

lets are provided. (Perhaps because of its low use, this site may be closed for periods when the DNR's budget becomes gaunt; no services are available at those times.)

At this point, the Hale Passage loop route turns back to the north. You can opt to cross to Portage Island for the return if currents will be against you, as they probably will be slower along the shallow eastern shore of Hale Passage. Portage Island, part of the Lummi Indian Reservation, is quite wild, with beaches fronting on woods and meadows beyond. Landings are prohibited for non-tribal members without permission. The island is connected to the mainland by a spit that dries at midtide, and cars frequently drive across it.

Lummi Island Circumnavigation: *Exposed.* The total paddling distance is approximately 19 miles. The portion from Gooseberry Point south along Hale Passage is described above. The description continues south from Lummi Island Recreation Site.

Venturing south toward Carter Point and around to the southwest side of Lummi Island takes you into a world of unforgiving rocky shorelines and steep, narrow beaches backed by talus slopes. There are few opportunities for anything but an uncomfortable emergency bivouac should the weather turn against you. After rounding the point, the shore is a continuous scree slope punctuated by cliffs that rise abruptly to the ridge line, which gradually ascends toward 1,600-foot Lummi Peak as you move north. There are few haulouts until opposite Lummi Rocks, and then the country gradually flattens, and some pastoral and residential developments appear, though most are kept at bay from the shore by bluffs.

Lummi Rocks, owned by the Bureau of Land Management and leased to Western Washington University for research and education, is a nice spot for a lunch stop and a stroll over its grassy knolls. There are no facilities here, and camping is not recommended.

Chuckanut Bay

The rocks make this Bellingham-area trip: the convoluted hollows and delicate lacework of saltwater-eroded Chuckanut sandstone formations, the fossilized remnants of ancient palm trunks, even a long-gone artist's sculpture on a seaside rock.

DURATION: Part day to full day.

RATING: Protected or Moderate. The longer Moderate route is exposed to southerly seas, and rocky shores could make landings difficult if the weather takes a bad turn.

NAVIGATION AIDS: NOAA charts 18424 (1:40,000) or 18423 SC; Port Townsend tide table (add about 45 minutes) for launch at Chuckanut Park.

PLANNING CONSIDERATIONS: The shorter excursion from Chuckanut Bay is feasible only at high tide.

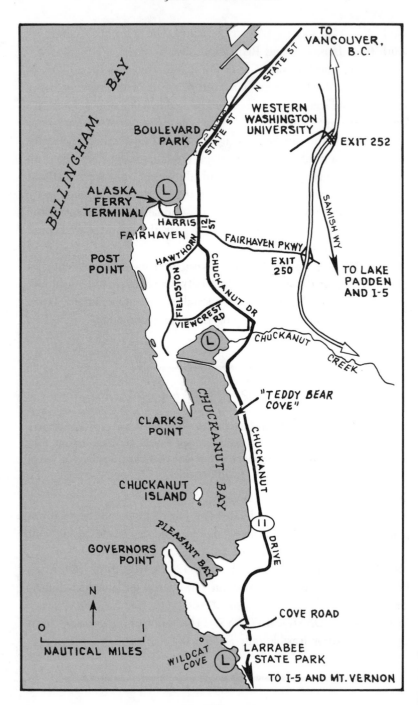

Getting There and Launching

The three launch points are accessible from Highway 11, also called Chuckanut Drive.

The northernmost is the Harris Street boat ramp in Fairhaven (really part of south Bellingham). Take Harris Street west from Highway 11 0.25 mile and turn right just before Fairhaven Boatworks. Keep right outside the chain-link fence to the boat ramp. Kayaks are available for rental next door.

Chuckanut Park is located in a cove in the northern part of Chuckanut Bay and provides the only access for the Protected route in the bay. However, this cove dries to extensive mud flats, so high-tide use is required. Follow Highway 11 1.5 mile south from Fairhaven to 21st Street. In 0.4 mile the road dead-ends at the water's edge, where there is limited parking. There are no facilities at this park.

Wildcat Cove, about 1 mile south of Chuckanut Bay, is part of Larrabee State Park. Follow Highway 11 south from Fairhaven 5 miles to Cove Road. Follow it downhill, turn left after crossing the railway, and go straight into the boat launch area. Launch on the gravel beach next to the boat ramp.

Routes

Chuckanut Bay: *Protected*. Make loops as long or short as you like, stay within the shallow cove at Chuckanut Park or paddle up to 4 miles around the entire bay. With the exception of the park and Chuckanut Island, all shorelines are private (some are Burlington Northern right-of-way). There are fine rocks to view within the cove before paddling under the railroad bridge to the larger bay. Clarks Point has a very attractive inner bay with four fossilized palm-tree trunks in the rocks, which are easily examined from your boat. Across Chuckanut Bay east of Clarks Point is a rocky outcrop and some small beaches along the railroad. The area is known as Teddy Bear Cove; Bellingham-area residents use it as a nude sunbathing and swimming area.

Chuckanut Island is owned by The Nature Conservancy, which allows stops ashore but no camping or fires. There are no facilities on the island, and they ask that you stay on the trail that rings the island. At high tide a small beach on the southwest side is the best landing, with a steep scramble to the island above. On lower tides, beaches on the north and southeast are uncovered. The latter surrounds interesting rocks but lacks access to the upper island.

Fairhaven to Wildcat Cove: *Moderate.* This 5-mile trip is best done with a 6-mile car shuttle between the Harris Street boat launch and Wildcat Cove (shortened 1 mile by a high-tide launch at Chuckanut Park). The Fairhaven end begins with a tour of shipyards and the southern terminus of the Alaska Marine Highway. Just past the shipyard is a marine park with rest rooms and a beach that is best for landings on lower tides.

To the south, the railroad parallels the shore, with two small embayments behind it that can be reached under low bridges (the second provides an exciting sluice under the bridge at midtide). Beyond, watch for a rock just above high tide that a sculptor rendered many years ago. Add as much of Chuckanut Bay as you like to the route (see Protected route above for features). South of Governors Point, which defines the south end of Chuckanut Bay, the eroded rocks take on a delicate lacy quality.

Fossil palm trunk, Chuckanut Bay

James Island

Rugged James Island State Park has plenty of trails and enough secluded coves to keep you busy for more than an overnight stay. For variety coming and going, there are two ways to get there from Lopez Island. And if you feel up to it, you can make the exposed Rosario Strait crossing from Fidalgo Head to James Island and avoid San Juan Island ferry hassles. This trip could be combined with one to Obstruction Pass (see the Obstruction Pass chapter) and Doe Bay, perhaps with a circumnavigation of Blakely Island.

DURATION: Overnight.

RATING: Moderate or Exposed. The Moderate route involves some currents and possible tide rips. The Exposed route requires a 3-mile open-water crossing with currents, tide rips, and shipping traffic.

NAVIGATION AIDS: NOAA Charts 18423 SC, 18421 (both 1:80,000), or 18430 (1:25,000); Rosario Strait current tables with corrections for Thatcher Pass.

PLANNING CONSIDERATIONS: Currents affect ease of travel and safety on both routes. See specifics about each.

Getting There and Launching

The alternative approaches begin from the Anacortes area (Washington Park on Fidalgo Head) or Lopez Island (Spencer Spit State Park).

For the Washington Park launch site, continue west through Anacortes approximately 4 miles, following signs to the San Juan Islands ferry. At the top of the hill above the ferry terminal, continue straight at the Y intersection where ferry traffic bears right and go another 0.5 mile to Washington Park. To get closest to the beach, drive down to the day-use parking area to unload at the gravel beach, then move your car to Lot B at the Y intersection behind the park entrance sign.

Starting from Lopez Island requires driving a car aboard the ferry, as there is no public access to the beach at the Lopez Island ferry terminal for foot passengers with kayaks. Drive south from the ferry landing a little more than 1 mile to Port Stanley Road (across the highway from Odlin County Park). Turn left and follow this road for approximately 3 miles as it winds past Shoal and Swift bays. Turn left onto Baker View Road and follow this road another mile to the state park entrance.

Within Spencer Spit State Park, use the gravel road to the right at the park office to reach the beach. This narrow road drops steeply to a small lot just south of the lagoon. There is a 50-yard carry to the beach. After unloading boats and gear, move cars back up to the main road, then go right to the parking lot and park just past the rest room on the left. The ranger asks that you leave a "float plan" with him or on your car in case of emergency.

Routes

Spencer Spit to James Island: *Moderate.* One-way paddling distance via Thatcher Pass is 4 miles, or 7 miles via Lopez Pass around the south end of Decatur Island.

Currents west of Blakely Island are weak, and the waterway there is fairly well protected from wind-driven seas. However, Eastsound, to the north and almost bisecting Orcas Island, can develop very strong, intensified northerly winds that may extend south as far as this route on warm fair-weather afternoons. Currents in Thatcher Pass rarely exceed 1 knot, and it can usually be paddled safely in any stage of the tide. However, currents are strong enough to be worth coordinating with the flow direction. The flood current flows west through Thatcher Pass.

The longer alternative route, looping south around Decatur Island, offers narrow inter-island passageways to thread through and views of this quiet and pastoral island (as with Blakely Island to the north, there is no public ferry service). Places to go ashore here include a small undeveloped island state park just north of the spit east of Lopez Pass, and extensive publicly owned tidelands (though all lands above are private). Examples are the shores of Center Island (which has some gravel pocket beaches) and over 2 miles of sand and gravel beach on the east side of Decatur between Lopez Pass and Decatur Head (with one intermediate strip of private tideland). The shore break here can be quite large when a southerly wind is blowing.

James Island has three camping areas (with multiple sites at each), a network of trails over its steep, rocky hills, and a secluded beach on the south shore. Its drawback is the rapacious raccoon population that

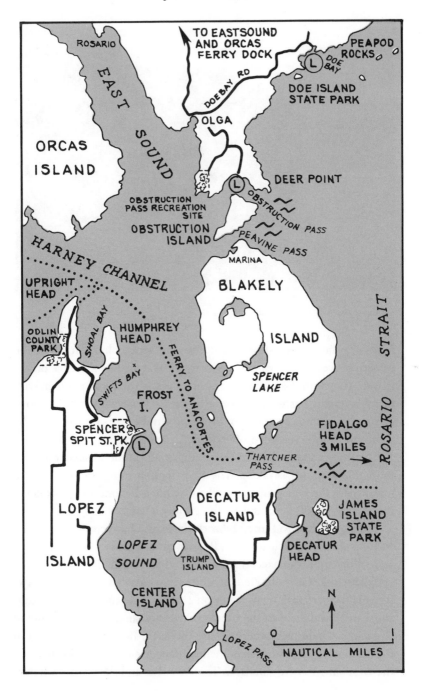

Southern shore of James Island

lurks in wait for all visitors. Campsites are accessible from either the eastern or western coves. A fee is charged. Water is not available on the island. The central area between the coves is the most popular with boaters, and it has a small picnic shelter. However, wind can howl across this isthmus from either direction. On the east side, camps at the southern side of the cove offer more protection.

The three secluded sites at the southern side of the west cove are the most popular with kayakers. The trees that surround these sites also make them the best protected in bad weather. Beyond the pit toilet, a trail leads across the island to the eastern cove.

Fidalgo Head to James Island: *Exposed.* One-way distance is 3.5 miles, 3 miles of which are open Rosario Strait waters. Currents in this area of the strait can exceed 2.5 knots and are usually strongest on the ebb, which flows south. Hence, southerly winds can make this an extremely dangerous body of water on a falling tide, and tanker and tug-and-barge traffic add to the hazard. Crossings should be made only in auspicious conditions; otherwise use the ferry. Be especially careful in the area north of James Island, where dangerous rips can form when the westward-flowing ebb from Thatcher Pass and the southward current in the strait meet an opposing wind. One kayak fatality here (following a Rosario Strait crossing) was apparently due to this situation. NOAA chart 18423 SC provides the following warning for Rosario Strait, presumably applying to Thatcher, Lopez, Peavine, and Obstruction passes: "On the ebb tide, southerly winds cause dangerous tide rips off the entrance to the passes."

If conditions and your skills seem appropriate for the Rosario crossing, time your start relative to the currents. Since your drift from the current will be considerable in all but very small tides, start the crossing about 30 minutes before slack so that the currents will be minimal and will cancel each other out before and after the slack. They are particularly swift off Fidalgo Head.

Obstruction Pass

Convoluted shores and steep hillsides of madrona and rocky meadows make Obstruction Pass prime San Juan Islands paddling country. Currents in its passageways are strong enough for some exciting rides, but also require a measure of caution. Alternative launch points around this area make a variety of trips possible, from short local paddles to overnight or longer. By adding another day to the itinerary, you could combine it with the Cypress Island route to the west or the James Island route to the south (see the Cypress Island and James Island chapters).

DURATION: Part day to overnight.

RATING: Moderate. Area has currents with associated tide rips and eddy lines, though the areas of swiftest flow can be avoided.

NAVIGATION AIDS: NOAA Charts 18423 SC, 18421 (both 1:80,000), or 18430 (1:25,000); Rosario Strait current tables with corrections for Obstruction Pass.

PLANNING CONSIDERATIONS: See the Fidalgo Head to James Island route in the James Island chapter for safety considerations in the passes leading to Rosario Strait, including Obstruction Pass.

Getting There and Launching

Launch from Lopez Island at Spencer Spit (see the James Island chapter for details) or from two alternative places on Orcas Island.

The closest launch site is the Obstruction Pass boat ramp. This site is approximately 20 miles from the Orcas Island ferry dock by road. After leaving the ferry, follow the road to Eastsound and then to Olga. Approximately 0.25 mile before Olga, turn left (signs point to Obstruction Pass and Doe Bay). After another 0.25 mile there is a fork in the road; go right for Obstruction Pass and left for Doe Bay. Use this ramp only for day-trip paddling; there is no overnight parking for the general public here.

Doe Bay Village Resort is the other Orcas Island alternative. See the Clark Island chapter for details about launching and other services offered at Doe Bay.

Routes

Spencer Spit to Obstruction Pass: *Moderate.* One-way distance is 4 miles. After crossing from Spencer Spit and Frost Island, this route follows the rocky shores of Blakely Island. The uplands of this large island are privately owned, but most of its tidelands are public. To avoid conflicts with residents, avoid landing in the coves along the western shore or near homes elsewhere. There are a number of fine, secluded gravel beaches along its predominantly wild shores. Stay below the high-tide line.

Blakely Island Marina at the west end of Peavine Pass has the only groceries on this route. The store operates on limited hours during the off-season. Land on the beach to the left of the fuel float.

Obstruction Pass Recreation Site provides camping and a chance for some walking on the extensive trail system. Located in a cove about 0.5 mile west of the pass, it is also accessible from the road via a 0.5-mile-long trail. Above the pebble beach are primitive campsites and pit toilets, but no water.

Unless you are confident of your boat-handling skills for fast currents, use Obstruction Pass instead of Peavine Pass for travel to and from Rosario Strait. Currents in Obstruction Pass average about 1 knot; they average over 2 knots on the ebb in Peavine Pass. Both flow east on the flood (toward Rosario Strait). Interestingly, this is *opposite* from the flow in Thatcher Pass (which is westerly on the flood).

Doe Bay to Obstruction Pass: *Moderate.* One-way distance is 4 miles. This and the previously described route from Spencer Spit could be combined into a longer 8-mile (each direction) overnight trip, though traveling into the San Juans by ferry the day before would probably be required to leave enough time for paddling.

Doe Island is a six-acre state park located about 1 mile south of Doe Bay. It has a float during the summer season, and rock and gravel beaches on the northwest and southeast sides. There are two campsite areas; the best is in a hollow on the north end of the island. No water is provided.

The Orcas Island shoreline is private between Doe Bay and Deer Point, though most of the tidelands are public with occasional gravel pocket beaches along the predominantly rock coast. You should be able to find beaches away from nearby homes.

Blakely Island Circumnavigation: *Moderate.* Distance (starting at Spencer Spit) is about 12 miles (8 miles of which are from Obstruction Pass to Spencer Spit via the east side of Blakely Island). A leisurely two-night trip could be made by a second stop at James Island.

The eastern leg of the circumnavigation is significantly more exposed, with fewer places to go ashore, strong currents, probable tide rips, and exposure to wind waves from either north or south. Tidelands are public along the entire east shore of Blakely Island; steep, rocky slopes above limit the residential use of this side but also limit the number of pocket beaches you will find. There may also be shore break on these beaches (be especially watchful for breaking tanker wakes). A powerful eddy line and associated tide rips may form during strong ebb currents in Rosario Strait at the easternmost point of Blakely Island. The current here is reported to turn to the flood an hour later than at Strawberry Island to the east. See the discussion of potentially dangerous conditions off Thatcher Pass and Peavine Pass for the Fidalgo Head route in the James Island chapter.

Jones Island

Sandy beaches, trails that meander through madrona groves and meadows, and a resident deer herd that mingles with campers make Jones Island one of the most popular San Juan Islands destinations for kayakers. Other boaters enjoy it too, and campsites may be scarce on summer weekends. For ferry foot-passengers with kayaks, this trip offers route alternatives using two ferry stops or round trips to and from Shaw Island or Friday Harbor. This area can also be combined with a circumnavigation of Shaw Island (see the Shaw Island chapter).

DURATION: Overnight.

RATING: Moderate. Involves a 0.5-mile open-water crossing in currents up to 2 knots.

NAVIGATION AIDS: NOAA charts 18423 SC or 18421 (both 1:80,000), and 18434 (1:25,000); San Juan Channel current tables or the Canadian *Current Atlas* in particular are useful for route timing with favorable flows.

PLANNING CONSIDERATIONS: Arrive early to secure a campsite on summer weekends. Coordinate with currents in Wasp Passage, Pole Pass, and (if Friday Harbor is a trip terminus) San Juan Channel.

Getting There and Launching

Take the San Juan Islands ferry to either Orcas, Shaw, or San Juan Island, depending on the launch site to be used.

Orcas Island's launch sites provide the closest access to Jones Island. If you have a car, driving to Deer Harbor to launch reduces the one-way paddling distance to Jones Island to about 2 miles. Water access is at Deer Harbor Marina and Resort, which charges a fee to launch and to park.

Launching at the ferry landing at Orcas is most practical for foot passengers, as parking is limited. There is no public access to the water; use Russell's float (a fee is charged) just west of the ferry dock.

The launch site at the Shaw Island ferry dock also is more appropriate for foot-passengers than for kayakers who arrive with cars, as there is not sufficient room to park here. Launch at the beach just west of the

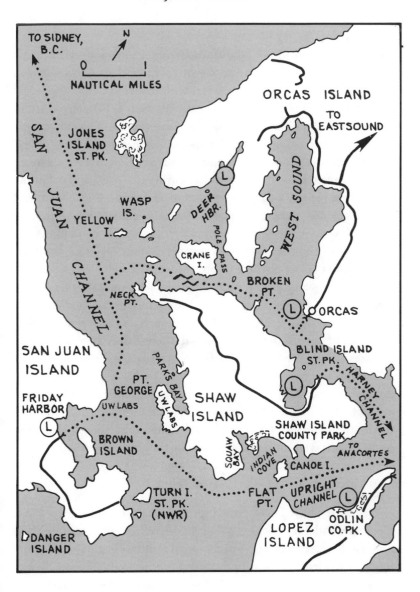

ferry dock. The Franciscan nuns operate a store at the landing that has a surprisingly extensive and interesting grocery selection.

At Friday Harbor, launch from the public dock a few hundred yards north of the ferry dock, using the floats nearest shore. Parking in Friday Harbor is extremely scarce during the summer.

Routes

Deer Harbor to Jones Island: *Moderate.* Paddling distance is just under 2 miles. Follow the western shore of Deer Harbor toward Steep Point, passing rocky shores covered with madronas, cliffs and occasional homes. All of the shoreline along this route is private, so plan to stay in your boat until reaching Jones Island. This route would qualify for a Protected rating, except for the Spring Passage crossing. Here, currents can reach almost 2 knots, and you may need to ferry upstream at a large angle to hold your position during the crossing. Seas in the passage can get quite rough when the wind opposes the current, and rips are possible. Hence, to be safest, time this crossing when currents will be flowing in the same direction as the probable wind direction.

Jones Island State Park is a very popular destination for kayakers and other boaters, so popular that campsites are difficult to find on summer weekends. Most boaters prefer the more protected northern cove, where there is a dock. Kayakers like the southern beach and a smaller one on the northwest side of the island, though southerly wind protection is slight at most of the campsites in these areas. There are numerous sites at both the northern and southern areas, and one on the west side. From the western beach, a 200-yard trail leads to the northern camp area. At all locations, only sites designated with a numbered picnic table may be used for camping. Pay the camping fee at the self-registration stations at the north and south ends. Though drinking-water faucets are provided at both places, the shallow well usually runs dry in midsummer, and the water is shut off between October and March (fees are not in effect at this time).

Orcas or Shaw Ferry Landings to Jones Island via Pole Pass: *Moderate.* Paddling distance is 4 or 4.5 miles from the Orcas or Shaw ferry landings, respectively. This is a good route for learning to use currents for efficient travel; with the possible exception of Spring Passage when wind opposes the current (discussed above), they are rarely fast enough to be hazardous but can substantially affect paddling effort. Currents in the passages between Shaw and Orcas islands generally flow westward during the flood tide and eastward during the ebb.

Pole Pass is a little tide race that can run at more than 2 knots for a short distance. It is rarely dangerous, but boat wakes in the riffles on the downstream side can make it quite rough. It is possible to go through against the current, as it is quite weak in the approaches. There are eddies to use on the Orcas Island side, and then a hard push is required for a short distance in the narrows against the flow. Be especially wary of boat traffic in Pole Pass, as it is difficult to see what is coming the other way as you approach.

With the exception of Blind Island State Park (see the Shaw Island chapter for details) just beyond the Shaw ferry landing, and public tidelands at Broken Point, there is no public access ashore along this route. However, it can be covered in less than two hours with favorable currents.

Orcas or Shaw Islands to Jones Island via the Wasp Islands: *Moderate.* Paddling distance is about 5 miles. This slightly longer alternative to the Pole Pass route makes a nice return from Jones Island, with a stop to see the unique flora at The Nature Conservancy's Yellow Island. The western end of this route is more exposed to southerly or northerly winds, so opt for the Pole Pass route if the weather seems chancy.

The Wasp Islands south of Jones Island, with scattered rocks and islets, make for interesting and scenic paddling. Most of the Wasp Islands are privately owned, and a few smaller ones are part of the San Juan National Wildlife Refuge, in which landings are prohibited.

Currents in this area are moderate. Wasp Passage runs swiftly enough to produce rips in the area of Crane Island. The major hazard here is the ferry, which takes this route between Friday Harbor and Orcas Island. It can come around the corner quite suddenly from either direction, so do not dawdle in midchannel at Wasp Passage and keep your group tightly together for all channel crossings. Also watch out for ferry wakes colliding with an opposing current (that is, when the ferry is traveling against the current), as these can become steep and nasty breakers. The wake will smooth out after entering the eddies along the sides of the passage.

The Shaw Island shore of Wasp Passage is a fine place to practice using shore eddies to travel against the current, if you need to do so. Note that the currents in this area run counter to what might be expected. They flow west into San Juan Channel on the flood tide.

Yellow Island, owned by The Nature Conservancy, is managed to perpetuate the island's floral communities. The main attraction is the spring flowers, which begin to bloom in late March and are at their best from mid-April through early summer. Resident caretakers live in the cabin on the southwest shore.

Kayakers should be aware that Yellow Island is *not* a public park, and that visits are permitted only under stringent conditions to ensure that the primary goal of preservation is not compromised. Stops here should be short and only for the purpose of viewing the island. Stay on the trail that meanders around it. Collecting plants or intertidal life, smoking, pets, camping, picnicking, and fires are prohibited, and there are no public toilets. The Nature Conservancy management has been concerned about kayakers using the meadows as toilets, and the island may be closed to kayak groups if the problem continues. Groups of more than six individuals must have prior permission to visit Yellow Island, obtained by calling The Nature Conservancy in Seattle at (206) 728-9696.

Friday Harbor to Jones Island: *Moderate.* The paddling distance is 4.5 miles. This alternative route is often used by kayakers who

Caretaker's cabin, Yellow Island

ride the ferries as foot-passengers, beginning their paddle to Jones Island at Shaw Island and reboarding the ferry for the return to Anacortes at Friday Harbor. Aside from Yellow Island (described above) there are no public shorelines along the route, but with favorable current and wind this trip should take less than two hours. Currents in this part of San Juan Channel can attain about 1 knot, so planning to use them is worthwhile.

The shoreline of Shaw Island is probably the more interesting side to follow (see the circumnavigation route in the Shaw Island chapter for details), and you can, perhaps cross to the San Juan Island side at Point George. Point George and Parks Bay behind it are part of a University of Washington biological preserve in which landings are not allowed.

At Friday Harbor, the public dock north of the ferry landing provides the closest place to the ferry to get ashore.

Shaw Island

Located in the heart of the San Juan Islands, the waters around Shaw Island usually have the highest concentration of kayaks in the area. Moderate currents and alongshore paddling with few crossings make some routes here popular for less-experienced paddlers, particularly those trying kayak-camping for the first time. Routes include an easy day or short overnight option (Upright Channel route) and a longer circumnavigation of Shaw Island, with stops at neighboring parks. The circumnavigation can easily include Jones Island (see the Jones Island chapter).

DURATION: Full day to two nights.
RATING: Protected or Moderate. The Moderate route involves currents and some open water that may become quite rough, particularly when current and wind direction oppose each other.
NAVIGATION AIDS: NOAA charts 18423 SC or 18421 (both 1:80,000), and 18434 (1:25,000). San Juan Channel current tables or the Canadian *Current Atlas* are helpful for the circumnavigation route; Port Townsend tide tables (add about 30 minutes) are handy if Indian Cove is included as a launch point or stop.
PLANNING CONSIDERATIONS: Timing with currents will greatly affect your speed and travel effort on the circumnavigation route. It is a

fairly complex task in this area, made easiest by the *Current Atlas*. Plan a high tide arrival or departure at Indian Cove to avoid the mud flats there. Campsites at Indian Cove and Jones Island are usually all spoken for on summer weekends, so arrive early.

Getting There and Launching

Either route can be started from Odlin Park on Lopez Island (a car is needed to reach this launch site from the ferry landing and there is no public water access at the ferry dock). Drive a little more than 1 mile south from the ferry terminal to Odlin County Park. There is easy access to the beach at the sandy beach. A campground is nearby. Cars may be parked for a daily fee paid to the caretaker at the residence near the entrance.

The circumnavigation route can also start and end at the ferry stops at Shaw Island, Orcas Island, or Friday Harbor, or from Deer Harbor. See the Jones Island chapter for a description of these launch sites.

Routes

Shaw Island Circumnavigation: *Moderate.* The total distance is approximately 14 miles. Add 2 miles for a side trip to Turn Island, 3 miles for Jones Island. Add 2 miles if you launch at Deer Harbor.

Five places to camp are distributed around and on Shaw Island (Blind Island, Jones Island, Turn Island, Indian Cove, and Odlin Park) and allow you to partition the trip into two or three fairly equal-length paddling days. This description begins at the Shaw Island ferry landing and proceeds counterclockwise around the island.

Blind Island State Park, about 0.5 mile west of the Shaw Island landing, is a convenient first-night stop for kayakers who take a late ferry into the islands. Facilities on this two-acre island are simple—a pit toilet, picnic tables, but no water. There is no fee for its three campsites. Landings can be made on rocky beaches at the southwest end or at the southeast corner of the island. Trees on the island are few, and the only wind protection is chest-high brush that shields some of the sites. Because it is small, Blind Island can become crowded with only a few parties camped there.

For the route west from Blind Island to Jones Island, including the Wasp Islands and Yellow Island, see the Jones Island chapter.

As you head east along Shaw Island's western shore, the San Juan Channel current can be quite strong, especially at the points that protrude into the waterway. There are eddy systems alongshore for much of the way, with extensive eddies in the vicinity of Parks Bay. Though most of the northern portion of this shore is developed with summer residences, there are some points of interest. The small islets north and south of Neck Point are very popular with seals—I have seen as many as 30 hauled out on the islands. Both islets are part of the San Juan Islands National Wildlife Refuge, so do not approach closer than 200 yards.

Beginning at Point George is a 1,000-plus-acre biological preserve, owned by the University of Washington, that extends south and west almost to Squaw Bay. Managed by the University of Washington Friday Harbor Laboratories, this preserve is off-limits to all public use in the uplands and tidelands. Nonetheless, you can still enjoy the forests and meadows as you paddle by.

Turn Island State Park, located a little over 1 mile south of Shaw Island across San Juan Channel, is a side-trip opportunity for camping or a break along this otherwise closed portion of the island circumnavigation. This island is a unit of the San Juan Islands National Wildlife Refuge. A portion of the west end is leased to the Washington State Parks and Recreation Commission. Camping is allowed only in this park area, with fees levied through the self-registration station. There are composting toilets, but no water is available. A rough trail circles the island. Keep in mind that public use of this refuge island is provisional on compatibility with wildlife, so avoid any nesting sites.

Be careful crossing San Juan Channel here. Currents are strong enough to require significant course adjustment to offset your drift, and steep seas can develop when the current opposes winds from either north or south. Watch for ferries and other heavy boat traffic associated with nearby Friday Harbor.

Travel in Upright Channel is described in the local route for that area (below). The Shaw Island shore north of Indian Cove is rocky and for the most part wild, and continues so west into Harney Channel. Currents in Harney Channel are stronger than in Upright Channel, but still pose few problems for travel. The flood current here flows west.

Upright Channel (Odlin Park to Indian Cove): *Protected.*
The round-trip paddling distance is about 4 miles. The most interesting route follows the Lopez shore south from Odlin Park to Flat Point, then heads across the 0.25-mile-wide narrows to Canoe Island and finally Indian Cove. You can return the same way, or make a loop by following the Shaw Island shore north along Upright Channel to cross opposite Odlin Park (about 1 mile of open water).

A little more than 1 mile south of Odlin Park is the Upright Channel Recreation Site, an undeveloped DNR parcel with no facilities. This 700-foot-long public gravel beach with forested uplands is located just east of the residences near Flat Point.

Watch carefully for boat traffic before crossing from the spit at Flat Point to Canoe Island, particularly the ferries going to and from Friday Harbor. Currents in Upright Channel generally are weak, but may have some force locally here (the flood flows north). Though Canoe Island beaches are public below mean high tide, the uplands are not and owners (who operate a youth camp specializing in French language and culture) strongly discourage visitors.

Shaw Island County Park, encompassing western Indian Cove and part of the peninsula that separates it from Squaw Bay, has opportunities for camping, picnicking, or more secluded stops ashore. Because the foreshore in Indian Cove dries for a considerable distance and becomes a muddy tide flat, plan around low tides for arrival and departure if possible.

Campsites are located along a road that starts near a low bank to the east and climbs as the bank increases to a bluff to the west. There are steps at intervals along the beach to the campsites, but the most westerly ones are not readily accessible from the water. Camping fees are per site for up to four people with an additional charge for more individuals. If you wish to share a site with others (and you may have to during peak weekends), there is a shared camp area just west of campsite 9, at a nominal charge per person. Water, pit toilets, and a cooking shelter are provided.

Take a short side trip west around the peninsula to Squaw Bay. The tip of this point is private land, but two pocket beaches on the west side make more secluded landing spots (though there is access from a spur road down the rocks from above the beaches).

South and West San Juan Island

Kayakers come here for two distinct reasons. The first is whales: Haro Strait is the best place to see orcas during the summer months. The state park at Limestone Point was developed primarily for public observation of the whales that pass offshore regularly. Second, the barren beauty of the largely treeless southwestern coast of San Juan Island is unique for the Northwest. The exposure to southerly and westerly winds and big seas along its beaches makes it the wilder. But to the north, western San Juan Island has a gentler face: inter-island channels and the accessible historical attractions of British Camp.

DURATION: Part day to multiple night.

RATING: Exposed or Moderate. Exposed routes involve strong currents and probable tide rips, characteristically strong winds with fully developed seas, and resulting surf on the beaches. See the description of wind patterns under the South Beach to Griffin Bay Route.

NAVIGATION AIDS: NOAA charts 18423 SC or 18421 (both 1:80,000) or 18433 and 18434 (both 1:25,000); San Juan Channel current tables.

PLANNING CONSIDERATIONS: Avoid mid- to late afternoon for paddling west of Cattle Point, when westerlies from the Strait of Juan de Fuca are strongest.

Getting There and Launching

There are many points of access here, but some car shuttling or walking will be needed unless you return to the launch point or commit to a 30-mile, multiday circumnavigation of San Juan Island. For the latter, kayakers who carry their kayaks aboard the ferries as foot passengers can choose Shaw Island (see the Shaw Island chapter for details) or Friday Harbor to launch (use the dinghy dock at the public wharf north of the ferry landing).

Starting from the north, Roche Harbor is a popular launch spot for a

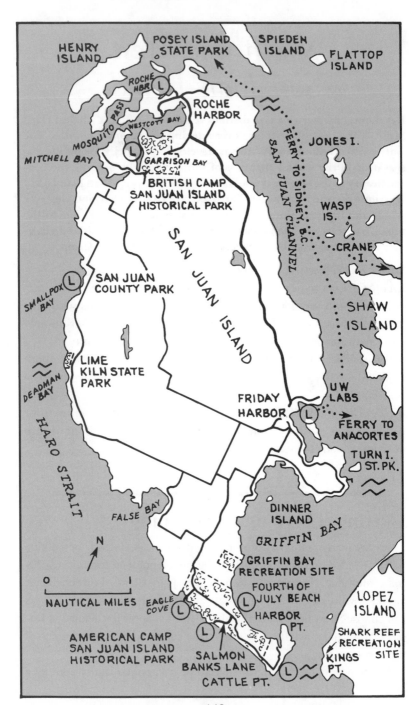

number of routes (see the Stuart Island chapter for directions and details on launching here).

British Camp is about 9 miles from Friday Harbor. From the ferry landing, follow Spring Street to Second Street, on the right. Follow this and go left where it becomes Guard Street. This in turn eventually becomes Beaverton Valley Road and then West Valley Road. Turn off to the left for the entrance to British Camp and go down the hill to the lot. Boats will have to be carried several hundred yards along gravel walkway and lawn (smooth enough for carts) to the sand and cobble beach. The park provides rest rooms and interpretive facilities that are open during the summer months.

Directions for San Juan County Park are the same, except that you turn left on Mitchell Bay Road about 7 miles from town. Turn left where it becomes the West Side Road and follow it to the park at Smallpox Bay. There is a lot with easy access to the gravel beach. Rest rooms and water are available.

Eagle Cove is located just north of the American Camp portion of San Juan Island National Historic Park. To reach the area from the Friday Harbor ferry landing, follow Spring Street three blocks to a Y intersection and go left on Argyle Street. This becomes Cattle Point Road and reaches the park after about 5 miles. Turn right onto Eagle Cove Road and go 0.5 mile to the parking lot. Boats must be carried 100 yards downhill on a sometimes slippery path to the gravel beach. This launch point will have more protection from surf than the beaches at Salmon Bank Lane farther south.

Traveling south in the park, the next launch spot is Fourth of July Beach, giving access to the southeast shore of the island in Griffin Bay. Turn left off Cattle Point Road 1 mile south of the park entrance and drive to the picnic area lot. The beach is a short distance below.

Salmon Banks Lane, with three parking lots giving easy access to continuous gravel beaches facing southwest, is reached by turning off Cattle Point Road onto Pickett's Lane a short distance south of the Fourth of July Beach intersection. Launches could be rough here in even a moderate wind.

Finally, Cattle Point Picnic Area gives access to the southern tip of the island. Continue past the point where you leave the national park for another 0.75 mile to the lot on the right. Boats must be carried 50 yards down rather steep rocks. Cattle Point itself gives some protection against surf at the west end of this beach.

Routes

South Beach (Salmon Banks Lane) to Griffin Bay via Cattle Point: *Exposed.* Paddling distance is 5 miles. This is the logistically easiest route, as the 1.5-mile walk between the launch and take-out points can eliminate the need for a car shuttle. A lunch stop could be taken at Cattle Point Picnic Area. Plan for plenty of time in Griffin Bay to explore the three lagoons there.

The Exposed rating is due to both currents and wind. Currents at San Juan Channel's south entrance can reach 5 knots, and heavy tide rips are likely, especially around Goose Island and Deadman Island on the Lopez Island side. Staying close inshore on the San Juan Island side may prove best. The current usually flows east off Cattle Point, as a large eddy forms there during the ebb cycle. This and the daily wind development pattern on fair-weather days suggest paddling from west to east. A flood current is most favorable.

The Haro Strait side of southern San Juan Island is exposed to southerly bad-weather winds, and is also a very windy area in fair weather. When there is a high-pressure area offshore, strong in-flow winds in the Strait of Juan de Fuca produce westerlies here up to 25 knots on fair afternoons, and are at their strongest from about 2:00 P.M. to 6:00 P.M. A little farther north in the strait, these become southwesterlies, and at the north end of San Juan Island, where the effects of the strait are less, northwesterlies. Pacific swells can penetrate through the Strait of Juan de Fuca, and together with local wind waves develop considerable surf on southwestern San Juan Island beaches, such as Salmon Bank Lane. Surf there is likely to be smallest in the morning on sunny days.

If wind makes travel west around Cattle Point imprudent, consider beginning at Cattle Point Picnic Area, cutting the paddling distance to 3 miles. There is plenty to explore in Griffin Bay—the three high-tide lagoons and a maze of old roads meandering through the woods above and between them. Or, add 2 miles to the route by paddling across the channel narrows to Lopez Island if currents are close to slack, including a stop at Shark Reef Recreation Site (undeveloped with no facilities), located just south of Kings Point.

Smallpox Bay (San Juan County Park) to Lime Kiln Point: *Exposed.* Round-trip paddling distance is 4 miles. This route can be paddled one-way with a 3-mile car shuttle to Deadman Bay (respect private property above the beach there), just south of Lime Kiln State Park.

This is the best coastline for whales. Facilities and interpretive displays at Lime Kiln State Park are geared toward whale watching. At least three separate pods (extended families) of orcas pass close by daily. Minke and pilot whales, Dall and harbor porpoise, and even an occasional gray whale are sighted here. Be sure to observe "orca etiquette" while paddling near them—don't approach within 100 feet or try to position yourself in their path of travel. If they are so inclined, they will come to you.

Shores along the way to Lime Kiln Point are largely rocky, with residences here and there. In a bight just north of the point are the old lime kilns, easily identified by the white piles of material on the hillside. To go ashore at the park, continue around the point and land on the north end of the beach at Deadman Bay.

Roche Harbor to English Camp via Mosquito Pass: *Moderate.* Round-trip paddling distance is 5 miles (or half that for one-way paddling with a 4-mile car shuttle). This entire route is very well protected from winds, and is an excellent route for most weather conditions. However, currents in Mosquito Pass are strong but erratic (there are no predictions for them). Paddlers not experienced with currents should stay close to the eastern side of the channel near Mosquito Pass. This is probably the easiest route for going through against the current. South of the Pass, turn left to enter even more protected waters in Garrison Bay. Land on the beach next to the blockhouse. There is a visitor center in the white barracks building just inshore from the blockhouse, and rest rooms are nearby.

Great San Juan Island Tour: *Exposed.* Circumnavigation distance is about 30 miles. Shorter partial circuits are: Cattle Point to Roche Harbor (17 miles) or Smallpox Bay to Friday Harbor (20 miles). Campsites around San Juan Island are sparse and irregularly spaced, with a 14-mile gap at the southwest portion. Choices include Turn Island State Park (just south of Friday Harbor—see the Shaw Island chapter for details), Griffin Bay Recreation Site, San Juan County Park at Smallpox Bay, or Posey Island (north of Roche Harbor—see the Stuart Island chapter for details).

The Griffin Bay campsite is located just south of Low Point, in a meadow area directly inshore from Halftide Rock. Water, pit toilets, and the single campsite are 400 yards inland at the trees. The grassy path is smooth enough for boat carts if you feel the need to keep your boat nearby. There is no formal access to this recreation site from the road.

San Juan County Park, in Smallpox Bay, is a very popular campground and generally full during the summer months. Fortunately, they have a reservation system. Information can be obtained by calling (206) 378-2992 or writing to the park at 380 Westside Road North, Friday Harbor, Washington 98250.

Cattle Point

Point Doughty
ORCAS ISLAND

Accessible only from the water, this little DNR Recreation Site at Orcas's northwest tip has attractive madrona and fir woods, tide pools, and spectacular cliffs (complete with a small sea cave or two) on the north side.

DURATION: Full day or overnight.

RATING: Moderate. A north wind can create rough conditions and surt along the Orcas north shore. Current and tide rips are likely off the point.

NAVIGATION AIDS: NOAA charts 18423 SC or 18421 (both 1:80,000), 18431 (1:25,000); Canadian *Current Atlas.*

PLANNING CONSIDERATIONS: Aim for times of least current to avoid tide rips while rounding Point Doughty.

Getting There And Launching

See the Patos, Sucia, and Matia Islands chapter for directions to the North Beach launch site.

Route

Round-trip distance from North Beach to Point Doughty is about 6 miles. Follow the beach west past occasional homes and small resorts. A mile short of the point, the shore begins to rise and interesting cliffs line the remaining distance. Rocks and shoals are extensive off the point and together with swift currents produce significant tide rips here. A close inshore route around the point may avoid them if the seas are smooth enough to allow it.

Unprotected moorage and a largely rock beach limit visits by other boaters, though the point is popular with scuba divers. Access is via a small beach on the south side of the point. At midtide or above, landings are on pebbles and gravel; low tide approaches are rocky and may be hard on the boat if there is a southerly sea running.

There are two campsites, pit toilets, and garbage cans, but no water.

One campsite has good views to the south and west, but poor weather protection. The other is tucked into the trees and is a good all-weather camp, but without views. Trails lead east from the campsites along the south bluffs and eventually to the YMCA's Camp Orkila, 1 mile to the east, though there is no public access by land.

Patos, Sucia, and Matia Islands

Separated by miles of sea from other islands in the San Juan group to the south and open to the expanse of the Strait of Georgia to the north, this chain of state park and wildlife refuge islands is famed for its intricate geology as well as its sometimes treacherous waters.

DURATION: Overnight or multiple night.

RATING: Exposed. Though this area is sometimes millpond smooth, it is also well-known for strong but erratic currents and big seas that develop from northerly winds on fair afternoons. **This is no place for inexperienced paddlers!**

NAVIGATION AIDS: NOAA charts 18423 SC or 18421 (both 1:80,000), or 18431 (1:25,000); Rosario Strait current tables or the Canadian *Current Atlas.*

PLANNING CONSIDERATIONS: Routes here put paddlers at the mercy of the weather and strong currents during long crossings, so consult forecasts and be prepared to lay over in the islands during bad weather. Currents are strong throughout the area but not reliably predictable (see the discussion in the North Beach to Sucia Island route).

Getting There and Launching

From the Orcas Island ferry dock, drive north to Eastsound. At Eastsound, turn north and drive to the end of the road at North Beach. Launch from the gravel beach at the North Beach road end. No overnight parking is allowed along the road. The Captain Cook Resort permits parking and boat launching for a daily fee.

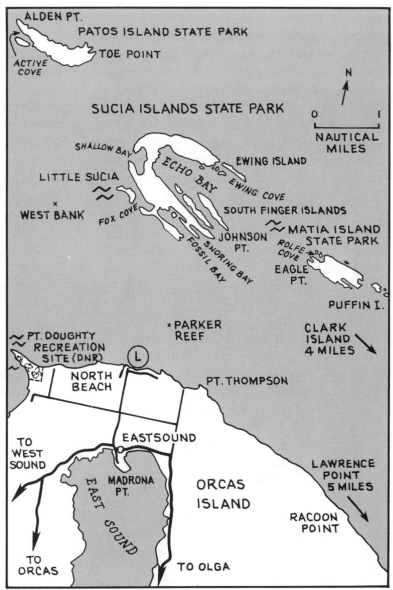

Routes

A weekend trip from North Beach to Sucia Island (about 5 miles round-trip), with an optional excursion to Matia (add another 2 miles) is one of the most popular kayak outings in the San Juan Islands. Including

Patos Island in the agenda adds another 5 miles or more to the total distance and usually merits another overnight on that island.

North Beach to Sucia Island: *Exposed.* Round-trip distance is about 5 miles, depending on your destination on Sucia Island. The crossing from North Beach to the nearest point on Sucia Island is 2 miles. The greatest hazard en route is Parker Reef, which consists of two separate shoals located less than halfway across. The area around the reefs can develop dangerous rips in strong currents (which can exceed 2 knots), made worse by contrary winds. In September, 1985, a kayaking fatality occurred there (reported in *Sea Kayaker* magazine, Winter 1985).

Generally, the west-flowing ebb current is considered the most dangerous. The Canadian *Current Atlas* shows the flood currents coming around the east and west sides of Orcas Island, meeting and weakening in this area. Timing of these currents is somewhat unreliable, and there have been reports of slacks varying greatly from their predicted times. (Using the *Current Atlas,* I once found the current flow to be the reverse of what was predicted.)

Nonetheless, this route attracts large numbers of paddlers during the summer months, novices included, to the point that I hesitated in giving it the Exposed rating. However, the potential for risk remains (as the record unfortunately shows), and so does my rating. More than a few first-time kayakers have had bad experiences between Sucia and Orcas, and some have been lucky to escape with their lives.

Sucia Island is the hub of cruising in the northern San Juan Islands, for yachts and kayaks alike. You are least likely to find solitude in the summer on Sucia Island, but other attractions make up for it. This island complex (actually at least six separate islands) can absorb a day's exploring by kayak (avoid Little Sucia Island, which is managed as an eagle preserve), and then another by foot along the extensive trail system. The bizarre formations of water-dissolved rock are unsurpassed, and seals abound on and around them.

The majority of visitors to Sucia Island are found in Fossil and Echo bays, where there are extensive campsites with drinking water and solar composting toilets. The low banks and shell and gravel beaches make attractive camping for kayakers in Fossil Bay or in adjoining Fox Cove. Echo Bay and Shallow Bay just across the island to the west have similar camps, with drinking water near the picnic shelters in northern Shallow Bay.

While the Fossil Bay and Echo Bay complexes are the best campsites for the off-season (driftwood for fires piles up in Echo Bay during the winter), kayakers visiting Sucia Island during the summer generally prefer Ewing Cove or Snoring Bay for the relative isolation from other boaters and campers that these areas afford. Camp only at sites designated with a fire ring and/or a picnic table. Camping elsewhere is prohibited.

Since campsites are often full to capacity at Sucia on busy summer weekends, the park provides a reservation service for groups of campers in sites at Shallow Bay (parties of nine or more) and Snoring Bay (for six or more). There is a fee for making a reservation, which should be done at least two weeks in advance by calling the park at (206) 376-2073.

North Beach or Sucia Island to Matia Island: *Exposed.* The crossing from Orcas to Matia Island is slightly longer (2.5 miles) and may involve strong currents (though the problems of the shallows at Parker Reef are easier to avoid).

Located little more than 1 mile from Sucia Island, Matia Island is hard-pressed to maintain its wild quality in the face of nearby boating activity. In fact, management of the island is something of a dilemma. Matia Island is entirely owned by the federal government as a national wildlife refuge managed for bald eagles and pelagic cormorants, with five acres at Rolfe Cove leased to the Washington State Parks and Recreation Commission (which in fact manages the rest of the island too for the U.S. Fish and Wildlife Service). Camping is confined to Rolfe Cove, which provides well-protected sites above the gravel beach and low bluffs. No water is provided on the island. A solar composting toilet is nearby. Fees are collected through the self-registration station. Nearby Eagle Cove is outside the state park lease area and closed to camping. Exploring ashore should be confined to a trail loop that runs down the center of the island and returns on the south side.

Around Matia Island are numerous coves best visited by boat to comply with refuge objectives of least on-shore disturbance. On the south side is the "hermit's cove," where remnants of a solitary island dweller's structures dating to the 1920s still can be seen. At the south-

Ewing Cove, Sucia Island

east corner are coves with pebble beaches. Refuge managers ask that you avoid the cove at the east end of the island (facing Puffin Island) because of eagle nests located there. Keep at least 100 yards distance from Puffin Island to avoid disturbing that refuge.

North Beach or Sucia Island to Patos Island: *Exposed.* From North Beach, Patos Island could be reached by following the Orcas shore west to Point Doughty, and then crossing slightly over 4 miles of open water, with strong currents and possible tide rips along the route. The safer but longer alternative is to head for Sucia Island first, and then cut across to Patos Island at the time of the slack. Both routes are safer and far easier on the flood current. Watch for rips in the area of West Bank (which is marked by an extensive kelp bed).

Patos Island is one of the wildest islands in the northern chain. The island is currently owned by the federal government and managed by the Washington State Parks and Recreation Commission, though a transfer to the state is forthcoming. Four acres at Alden Point will remain a Coast Guard light station and are off-limits to the public.

All recreational use is confined to the west end of the island, as the remainder is managed to enhance bald eagle nesting habitat, and the DNR is designating the eastern end as a Heritage Area for the preservation of plant communities there. Campsites are located at Active Cove, with pit toilets but no water or garbage service (and no charge for their use).

Patos Island does merit a circumnavigation, taking care to avoid disturbing the eagles along the way. On the south shore are bluffs and low cliffs, with the weirdly eroded conglomerate rocks that characterize this island chain. The east end has two coves with pebble beaches and long rock reefs, which are revealed at low tide a long distance from shore, giving Toe Point its name. These beaches characterize the majority of the northern shoreline.

Great Rectangle Route: *Exposed.* Paddling distance is about 25 miles. This string of Patos, Sucia, and Matia islands could be integrated into a large box route including Clark Island (see the Clark Island chapter), with the other side formed by the entire north shore of Orcas Island. Camping could be at the three islands described above, at Clark Island, or at Point Doughty on northwestern Orcas Island (see the Point Doughty chapter). Plan on two or (better) three nights for this trip.

Getting from Matia Island to Clark Island involves a 4-mile crossing, and the active currents between Clark and Orcas islands make both crossings precarious in unfavorable conditions (the Clark Island chapter includes a description of currents between Clark and Orcas islands). In unsettled weather, I recommend cutting this area out of the rectangle.

The north shore of Orcas Island forms the return leg of the rectangle route. Though this 6-mile-long linear shoreline between Lawrence Point and North Beach appears unexciting on the chart, I found it gratifying to follow. There are few spots for an emergency camp, so hope for fair weather during this leg of the journey. Most of the shore is very steep, with either wooded scree slopes or cliffs rising right from sea level. There are occasional narrow gravel beaches at the base but rarely anywhere to go above. Nonetheless, the coast is wild—look for otter and hauled-out seals—and has a few surprise bits of history. At one point there is an old limestone kiln fitted into the steep slope, so unobtrusively that most other boaters probably miss it. Farther on is an extensive, overgrown quarry now covered by a vigorous young fir forest.

Near the tiny extension of Moran State Park that reaches the sea is a rarity for the San Juan Islands—a waterfall spilling into the sea at high tide. Houses appear during the final third of the way to North Beach.

Clark Island

Because moorings here are somewhat exposed, Clark Island gets fewer overnight boaters than other state park islands in the northern San Juans. But ashore, kayakers will find that this little jewel includes paths winding through madrona along its shores, a gravel beach on one side and sand on the other, and extensive tide pools to explore. Its location allows radically different approach routes. The southern route—from Doe Bay on Orcas Island—is the shorter, though it requires a ferry ride from the mainland. The launch point at Doe Bay Resort offers opportunities to camp, rent a cabin, or just take a soak in their hot tubs on the way home. The northern route originates in the Lummi Indian Reservation between Bellingham and Ferndale. Few kayakers think of this northeastern approach to the San Juans, which has some significant advantages.

Clark Island

DURATION: Full day or overnight.

RATING: Exposed. Both routes require 1.5- to 2-mile crossings through a strong current with possible shipping traffic on the northern route. Tide rips are likely along either route.

NAVIGATION AIDS: NOAA charts 18423 SC or 18421 (both 1:80,000), or 18430 (1:25,000); Rosario Strait current tables with local corrections or the Canadian *Current Atlas.*

PLANNING CONSIDERATIONS: For the southern route, aim for times of least current in the area between the north shore of Orcas Island and Clark Island. (See the discussion of the behavior of the eddies in this area and accompanying hazards below.) For the approach from Gooseberry Point and Lummi Island, plan for times of minimal current in Rosario Strait and avoid flow conflicting with the likely wind direction. Currents in this area have no precise secondary reference station in the NOAA current tables. (The station 1.5 miles north of Clark Island is the closest.) The Canadian *Current Atlas* is most useful for gauging the timing and strength of the current on this crossing.

Getting There and Launching

To reach Doe Bay Resort from the Orcas Island ferry landing, follow Orcas–Olga Road north to Eastsound and then to Olga—about 16 miles. Turn left on Olga–Point Lawrence Road and go another 4 miles to the resort. Long a popular retreat for people with an inclination toward natural foods and living, Doe Bay's cabins, saunas and hot tubs are busy year-round. An area for tent camping is nearby. There is also a cafe and a natural-foods general store. The management asks a nominal fee to camp and launch there. A soak in the hot tubs is an additional fee.

See the Lummi Island chapter for directions to the Gooseberry Point launch. For Bellingham or Vancouver, B.C., residents, this northern approach is the most convenient access to the northern San Juans (for Sucia and Matia islands as well as Clark). Seattle-area dwellers wishing to access this northern San Juan Islands area will find that it takes less time to drive to Gooseberry Point than to ferry to Orcas Island, and it's certainly less expensive. During busy summer weekends, the time saved may amount to a half day or more due to San Juan Islands ferry traffic backups.

Routes

Doe Bay to Clark Island: *Exposed.* The distance from Doe Bay to Clark Island is about 4 miles. Though the shoreline of Orcas north from Doe Bay makes pretty paddling, consider a detour 0.5 mile offshore to the Peapod Rocks if weather permits and currents are favorable. This San Juan Islands National Wildlife Refuge unit (no landings permitted) has abundant bird life, seals, and sometimes sea lions. Remember to keep a distance of 200 yards from these and other refuge rocks.

Lawrence Point is DNR land, and though open to camping it is not a particularly good place for it. There are no facilities here. The grassy point does make a pleasant lunch stop or a place to watch the swirling currents and wait for favorable ones. Access is via two narrow pebble beaches on the south side of the point.

The 1.5-mile crossing to Clark Island from Lawrence Point can expose you to hazards created by strong currents. On both flood and ebb tides, large eddies form around Lawrence Point and powerful rips may occur at the boundaries with the main current streams. The Canadian *Current Atlas* gives the best picture of the complex flows in this area. Note that strong east-flowing currents move along the shore of Orcas Island on large flood exchanges in this area (the opposite of what you might expect) and flow the same way on large ebbs, too. The current can produce strong tide rips as it passes over a shoal (not shown on chart 18423 SC) just east of a line between Lawrence Point and Clark Island. Hence, time your crossing to the Lawrence Point area to arrive at slack time, and avoid this area on ebbs if southerly winds are likely. Because there are eddies near the point, a close-in route is safest if you must pass by while the current is running.

Gooseberry Point to Clark Island: *Exposed.* The paddling distance is approximately 7 miles each way. The shortest route is around the north end of Lummi Island; the south end makes a much longer but interesting alternative (add about 13 miles, with an overnight stop at Lummi Island Recreation Site—see the Lummi Island chapter for details). Begin with the 1-mile crossing of Hale Passage, where currents can be as strong as several knots. A flood current would be advantageous for reaching the north end of the island; you could gradually work across while the moving water carries you north. The Lummi Island shore is mostly residential until you round Point Migley, where bluffs conceal developments from the water.

The 2-mile crossing to Clark Island from Lummi Island's Village Point is exposed to the Strait of Georgia to the north and Rosario Strait to the south, and challenged by both swift currents (with possible tide rips) and busy shipping in Rosario Strait (particularly tankers en route to Ferndale's Cherry Point terminal).

Currents move very swiftly around both ends of Clark Island and nearby Barnes Island (privately owned), so watch out for tide rips. The Sisters Islands to the southeast of Clark Island are units of the San Juan Islands National Wildlife Refuge. Landings are prohibited; keep your distance to avoid disturbing the residents.

Paths circle the low bluffs around the southern end of Clark Island, with open madrona woods onshore and extensive tide pools and tide flats below at low tide. There are no trails to the brushy north end, but rounding the cliffs and offshore rocks makes a nice paddling excursion. There is a sand beach on the west side and a gravel one on the east. Sites on the west beach are for picnicking; camping is allowed on sites most easily reached from the east side.

Approximately six campsites are spaced out along the east beach and are low enough that a loaded kayak can be dragged over the smooth gravel right into camp. No water is provided on the island, nor is there a camping charge. The beach sites are vulnerable to bad weather; two sites in the woods at the narrowest point of the island are best at those times.

Stuart Island

I consider Stuart Island to be among the "wildest" of the San Juan Island trips, both because part of this area is dramatically natural and because the tidal forces are at their strongest here. This is no place for novices. You are likely to generate some excitement just paddling to and from Stuart Island, but its shorelines and two park areas are sure to make the visit a pleasure.

DURATION: Overnight or longer; two nights recommended.
RATING: Exposed. Strong currents and tide rips are likely throughout this area.
NAVIGATION AIDS: NOAA charts 18423 SC, 18421 (both 1:80,000)

or 18432 (1:25,000); San Juan Channel current tables with corrections for Limestone Point, Admiralty Inlet current tables with corrections for Turn Point, or the Canadian *Current Atlas*.

PLANNING CONSIDERATIONS: Currents in this area are very strong, and powerful rips form in all weather conditions. Coordination with currents is essential for both efficient travel and safety, particularly when there are larger-than-average tides.

Getting There and Launching

Launch at Roche Harbor or Friday Harbor, both on San Juan Island.

To reach Roche Harbor, drive from the Friday Harbor ferry landing two blocks through town to Second Street South, and turn right. After three blocks bear left on Guard Street, then right on Tucker Avenue. At the fork, bear left onto Roche Harbor Road. The total distance is about 10 miles.

Launching at Roche Harbor is allowed by the Hotel de Haro resort at the ramp or the adjoining grassy area about 100 yards south of the hotel (there may be a charge to launch here). Parking is in a pay lot across the street.

Alternative launch points include Friday Harbor, Orcas Island, or Shaw Island (see the Jones Island and Shaw Island chapters for the latter two).

To launch from Friday Harbor, use the public dock east of the ferry landing. Overnight parking is very limited and almost unobtainable in Friday Harbor during the summer (check in the port office at the public dock for possibilities).

Routes

Roche Harbor to Stuart Island: *Exposed.* The round-trip paddling distance is 10 miles. This is the shortest, least hazardous, and most popular approach to Stuart Island. Add 10 miles to the round-trip distance if launching from Friday Harbor.

Paddling between San Juan Island and Stuart Island probably requires more careful timing with the currents than anywhere else in the

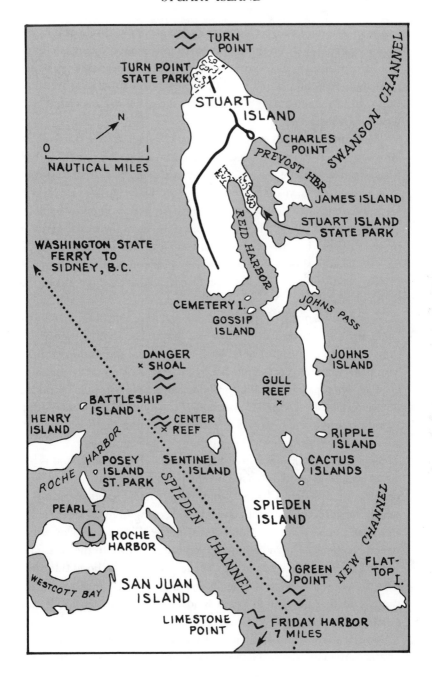

San Juan Islands. Though the crossings are generally 1 mile or less, the strong currents that run through these channels and the associated tide rips earned this trip its Exposed rating. However, since tidal cycles are predictable, careful planning and timing can make this a safer trip than those with the same rating due to longer crossings and associated bad-weather exposure.

The primary hazards occur in Spieden Channel. At the eastern end, between Green Point on Spieden Island and Limestone Point on San Juan Island, is some of the fastest water in the San Juan Islands; it runs over 5 knots on the year's biggest tides. Most significant are two powerful and extensive tide rips that form off both points on both the flood and ebb sets of the tide. The rip off Limestone Point forms 100 yards or more offshore, but the Green Point rip extends in quite close to Spieden Island's shoreline. There are less severe rips at the western end of the channel in the vicinity of Danger Shoal, Center Reef, and Sentinel Island.

The channels north of Spieden Island, on either side of the Cactus Islands, also run very swiftly, though you will find no local reference stations for them in the current tables. Currents here and in the northern San Juan Channel are somewhat fickle, particularly after the tide changes when patterns of flow around each side of San Juan Island are not yet established. One kayaker bound for Jones Island from Flattop Island reported being carried to Spieden Island on the flood current, when it should have been flowing in the opposite direction.

Since the total distance from San Juan Island to Stuart Island is too far to paddle in a single slack-current period, give most low-current priority to Spieden Channel, and then round Spieden Island in whichever direction is most convenient (keeping in mind the possible rips close to Green Point). Currents in Spieden Channel are slower between Davison Head and Sentinel Island than farther to the east. This area might be a good place to start at the tail end of the flood tide, then ride the ebb current west along Spieden Island, and finally take advantage of that current to reach Reid Harbor, compensating to the northeast against its flow.

Most of the small islands and rocks north of Spieden Island are units of the San Juan Islands National Wildlife Refuge; do not approach them.

If you make a late start from Roche Harbor or run late on the return, tiny Posey Island State Park outside the harbor's two approaches makes a suitable overnight spot. As on other small islands in Washington's park system, there is one outhouse but no water. Three campsites are located on the south, east, and west sides, with wind protection from the trees and brush at the center depending on wind direction. Since Posey Island is close to Roche Harbor's many summer homes, you can expect company in the summer months from young party-makers who bring their music with them.

For camping at Stuart Island, both Reid and Prevost harbors are suitable for kayakers. Both are part of Stuart Island State Park, one of the few marine parks in the San Juan Islands where you can count on finding fresh water; the well rarely runs dry. The fee for camping is levied through a self-registration station.

Reid Harbor is my favorite for camping, particularly the sites on either side of the marsh at the head of the bay. The beach here dries for a fair distance—great for clam diggers but not so good for gear-laden kayakers on minus tides. The three or four campsites on either end of the beach have their own outhouses and water. Be advised that the walk to the self-registration station is long and arduous (0.5 mile up and over the steep hill to the north), whereas it is a 150-yard paddle to the dock just below it, so take care of this detail before you stash your boat.

There are sites above the dock at Reid Harbor, but the only access to the top of this steep shoreline is via the twisting dock ramp—not easy carrying for a kayak. Nonetheless, this access is easier for getting your craft across to Prevost Harbor or the campsites there than the four and 0.5-mile paddle via Johns Pass.

As in Reid Harbor, there are campsites above Prevost Harbor's dock and float. But here the bank is lower, and an easy path leads up from the beach next to the dock. The four sites about 100 yards west are especially appealing, as they have their own beach access. This area also has outhouses and a water faucet.

I strongly suggest allowing a day layover at Stuart Island for some exploration, perhaps to hike the island's ample trails and little-used, unpaved country roads. There are fine opportunities for day-long loops, each skirting the island from one harbor to the other via Johns Pass to the east or Turn Point to the west.

Turn Point

Whichever way you go, note that the currents flow around both ends of the island on their way to or from the Strait of Georgia. With the right timing, both trips can be made with favorable currents for almost the entire distance. See the Canadian *Current Atlas* for specifics.

Reid Harbor to Prevost Harbor via Johns Pass One-day Loop: *Protected.* The total paddling distance is 4.5 miles. The Johns Pass loop is easier and shorter than the Turn Point loop (below). Most of this shoreline is residential. Except for Johns Pass, currents along the shore usually are benign, hence the Protected rating. Tiny state-owned Gossip Island and Cemetery Island at Reid Harbor's entrance are the only opportunities for shore exploration along this route.

Reid Harbor to Prevost Harbor via Turn Point Loop. *Exposed.* The paddling distance is 7 miles. I consider the western circuit around Turn Point exceptionally appealing. The wild, rugged shores and boisterous Haro Strait waters provide a setting unmatched in our inland waters. But because of the steep shores with few safe landings, the strong currents that race around the point, and the open north or south fetches with potential for sea development, I rate this loop Exposed.

From Prevost Harbor, the pastoral civility of Stuart Island is left behind at Charles Point. From there to Turn Point is a progression of rocky kelp beds, sea crags, and overhanging vegetation. Extensive eddies occupy most of these beds all the way to the point, and progress is fairly easy even against the current. These waters are prime fishing grounds for both bottom fish and salmon.

Turn Point is a 10-acre Coast Guard light station reservation surrounded by a 53-acre state park. The light facility is now automated, and the lightkeepers' residences are only occasionally occupied by diverse tenants such as Stuart Island teachers or whale researchers. The park land is undeveloped, with no recreational facilities. Camping is not allowed. It does provide excellent day hiking, and is a popular 5-mile round-trip hike for boaters from the Reid and Prevost harbors area via an unpaved road.

Turn Point itself provides few easy landing sites for visiting the light station. Though the rocks have eroded into fairly flat shelves, you will have to be adept at landing on rocks in the waves that are usually present. Also beware of the powerful wakes of the ships that pass quite close offshore here.

A much more practical landing with a rough trail access to the point is found at a small gravel beach about 0.25 mile to the south, just beyond some spectacular sea cliffs and still within Turn Point State Park. Secure your boat well above the drift logs and passing freighters' wakes and plan to be gone for at least one hour if you intend to visit the point.

The rough, little-used trail switchbacks steeply up from the beach. Follow the gully above the beach uphill for about 100 yards to a more well-defined trail that climbs across the hillside to the left through open fir and madrona woods. This trends upward for another 300 yards, passing open, grassy meadows above and below, perfect for secluded sunbathing. Finally it reaches a high, bald hilltop with sweeping views over Haro Strait, Boundary Pass, and the Canadian Gulf Islands beyond. Walking down to the cliff edge, you can see Turn Point light below. A few yards behind this bald hilltop is the old road linking the light station to the Reid and Prevost harbors area. Follow it to the left and downhill to the point.

Isle-de-Lis Provincial Park, Rum Island

Gulf
Islands
(British
Columbia)

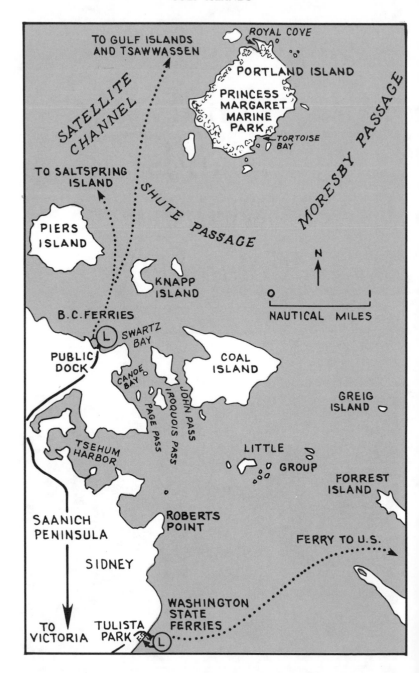

Portland Island
PRINCESS MARGARET MARINE PARK

Convoluted shores, lots of nearby islets, seemingly endless meadows lined with red-barked arbutus (known as "madrona" in the U.S.), and remnants of old orchards make this one of the jewels of the Gulf Islands. If you come here to camp, allow lots of time to explore the extensive trail system around and across the island. This excursion is easily integrated into the D'Arcy Island loop (see the D'Arcy Island Loop chapter) to the south for a multiple-night trip.

DURATION: Full day or overnight.

RATING: Moderate. Currents here can be strong enough to produce tide rips and rough seas when opposing wind. Boat and ferry traffic is heavy.

NAVIGATION AIDS: Canadian Hydrographic Service chart 3310 (small craft strip charts in folio) or 3441 (both 1:40,000); Canadian Hydrographic Service current tables (volume 5) for Race Passage with corrections for Swanson Channel, or Canadian *Current Atlas.*

PLANNING CONSIDERATIONS: This island receives heavy camping use, so arrive early to secure your site here on summer weekends. Travel with current flow (flood moves north).

Getting There and Launching

Launch sites at either Sidney or Swartz Bay are adjacent to (respectively) the Washington State (Anacortes) or B.C. ferry terminals, so follow signs to the appropriate one.

In Sidney, use the beach next to the launching ramp in Tulista Park, located just south of the Washington State Ferries terminal. If driving off that ferry, turn left after reaching the highway and then left again into the park in about 0.2 mile. Park in the area for vehicles launching boats. If walking off the ferry with your boat, follow the vehicle route around the terminal, except follow the paved path across the lawn immediately after passing the terminal—about 0.25 mile carrying distance. There is also a rough path to a narrow gravel beach in front of the

West side of Portland Island

terminal; turn toward the water just after exiting the terminal. This is a much shorter carrying distance, but space on the beach is limited at high tide and the shore break here may be much larger than behind the breakwater at the park.

At Swartz Bay, use the beach below the public dock just east of the terminal. If exiting the ferry by car, make a left turn where allowed soon after the terminal and follow the road back past the parking area. Turn left about 100 yards past the terminal onto a short street that dead-ends at the dock. Park along the street or if it's full, at the terminal. Foot passengers can take a shorter route (requiring a 0.25-mile carry) with their boats after leaving the ferry, cutting across the vehicle lanes to a gate at the main terminal building (below the "control tower") and going east through the parking area.

Route

One-way distance from Swartz Bay to Portland Island is 2 miles; it's 4 miles from Tulista Park in Sidney. Those originating from Sidney can sightsee through John, Iroquois, or Page passes, where sumptuous homes and moored yachts line the shores. Paddlers starting from either place should go east of Knapp Island to avoid the busy ferry lanes on the west side. Currents in Shute Passage flood northwest at up to 1.5 knots, and in the opposite direction at the same speed on the ebb, requiring a substantial ferry-angle course adjustment to control the amount that you are set by it. The Canadian *Current Atlas* is very helpful for timing with this current.

Portland Island has an extensive trail system and picnicking/camping facilities (tables and pit toilets) at several points along its shore. Water is available from a hand-operated pump in the center of the island. For orientation and access to water, stop at Tortoise Bay (called Princess Bay on some charts). There is a map here and at Royal Cove at the north end of the island. Boats moor at both of these locations and traffic ashore is heaviest there. Camping is best on the south and east-to-northeast sides of the island, accessible from beaches or eroded sandstone shores (the latter may be difficult in rough southerly conditions). If a fire ban is not in effect, campfires can be built in designated rings. Best to rely on your cook stove on this wildfire-prone island.

Pender, Saturna, and Mayne Islands

This part of the southern Gulf Islands offers the most opportunities for small-channel paddling, but with swift currents in some passages that are inappropriate for the inexperienced. There are many route variations here, especially for those who carry kayaks aboard the B.C. ferry and can use different island stops to begin and end the paddling trip.

DURATION: Part day to overnight.

RATING: Moderate. Currents in parts of this area are strong, with at least two local tide races (the most challenging one is avoidable).

NAVIGATION AIDS: Canadian Hydrographic Service chart 3310 (1:40,000 small craft strip charts in folio), or 3442 (1:40,000) and 3477 (1:15,000); Canadian Hydrographic Service current tables (volume 5) for Active Pass with corrections for Georgeson and Boat passages, current tables for Race Passage with corrections for Swanson Channel, or the Canadian *Current Atlas*.

PLANNING CONSIDERATIONS: Travel with current flows as much as possible. The flood goes northward in Pender Canal and northwest in Plumper Sound. These have no current predictions but can be estimated from those in Swanson Channel.

Getting There and Launching

Unless you integrate this trip with the Portland Island route to the west (see the Portland Island chapter), you will have to use the B.C. ferries to either Pender, Mayne, or Saturna islands. If coming from the mainland (Tsawwassen), you will have to transfer ferries at Mayne Island to reach Saturna Island (or at Swartz Bay if the schedule works out to be better).

Those who drive aboard can access the center of this paddling area via Pender Island, allowing a shorter and more sheltered route between the two Pender islands or across to Saturna. Launch at Browning Harbour public dock. To get there from the ferry landing, take Otter Bay Road east to Bedwell Harbour Road, turn right, and follow it to the intersection of Razor Point Road. Turn left and follow that about 1 mile to the public dock. Limited parking is available along the road.

Foot passengers can wheel their boats on and off at Mayne Island (Village Bay) or Saturna Island. At Village Bay, turn left immediately after leaving the ferry through a gate leading to a path to the beach. At Saturna Island, turn left to the public dock next to the ferry landing. A store is located just above the ferry dock at Saturna.

Routes

Options here are local paddling in Port Browning and Bedwell Harbour, up to a full day of exploring between Saturna and Mayne islands, or a longer overnight route that includes both of the above (camping at Beaumont Marine Park) and begins at Village Bay, either returning there or reboarding the ferry at Saturna Island for the return.

Port Browning-Bedwell Harbour: *Moderate +* . Round-trip distance is 4 to 6 miles. This could be a day trip or an overnight, with camping at Beaumont Marine Park, the only camping facility in this area.

This trip would fall within the Protected description were it not for the current in Pender Canal, which can run at up to 4 knots for a short distance under the bridge (there are no predictions about the current's schedule here, other than it flows north on the flood). This passage requires some care, but should be no problem for paddlers with average boat-handling skills. Whether going through with or against the cur-

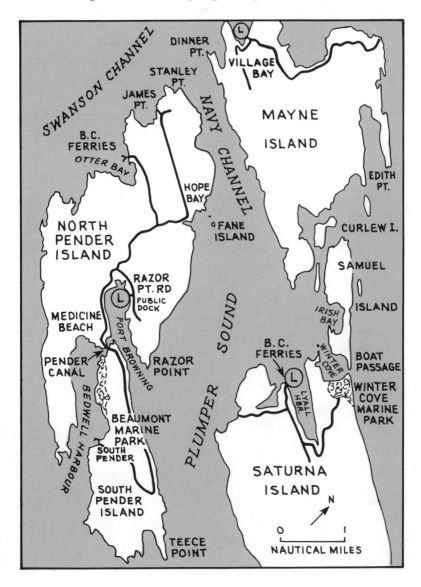

177

rent, look carefully for powerboats going through the cut, as they must maintain speed to have maneuverability in the current and have limited deep water in which to avoid you. Bigger boats going through against the current make large breaking wakes on the beaches. If you are going through against the flow, you may need to walk your boat under the bridge in the shallows, or carry it along the beach. You should be able to find eddies in both the north and south approaches to the canal.

The canal area, which was a portage until being dredged at the turn of the century, was a long-used Salish townsite, and an archaeological team dug here for a number of years. However, there was little ashore to see in 1989.

Beaumont Marine Park begins on the northern shore of Bedwell Harbour at Ainslie Point, and there are several nice beaches for a break

Boat Passage

ashore, with trails that connect with the developed part of the park farther south. The shell beaches there and shells in the soil above attest to the history of Indian use in the camping and picnic areas. Pit toilets, tables, and a water pump are the extent of the facilities.

About 1 mile farther south is South Pender, which has a customs station (open May 1 to October 1) and marina. At this writing, the facilities ashore had been sold and their future was uncertain.

Between Mayne and Saturna: *Moderate.* The distance from Saturna ferry landing can be as little as a 3-mile round trip to Winter Cove or lengthened to about a 7-mile circumnavigation of Samuel Island. A trip to Winter Cove avoids significant currents, but allows a close-up look at fast water in little Boat Passage, which can reach 8 knots. The east side of Winter Cove is a marine park that is restricted to day use. A gravel beach just east of Boat Passage gives access to trails for a view of the passage and the Strait of Georgia beyond.

Circumnavigating Samuel Island should be attempted only if you are comfortable with strong currents and sharp eddy lines, or if you plan to traverse its tide races at slack (especially Boat Passage). If your skills are up to it, Boat Passage can be run in midstream with few problems. Going through against the flow is difficult without portaging, as there are no eddies. Currents at the western end of Samuel Island are slower, but still provide challenging eddies and possible tide rips between Samuel and Curlew islands.

Village Bay–Winter Cove–Bedwell Harbor Triangle Loop: *Moderate.* Involves about 20 miles of paddling. Travel in the Pender Islands and between Mayne and Saturna is as described above. Use Swanson Channel predictions for Plumper Sound and Navy Channel, but note that Navy Channel floods east (maximum 3 knots) from Swanson Channel, meeting the west-flowing flood current from Plumper Sound off Hope Bay. Current speeds in Plumper Sound between Saturna and South Pender Island can reach 3 knots.

D'Arcy Island Loop

This loop avoids the more crowded cruising grounds of the Gulf Islands. With the exception of popular Sidney Spit, you are more likely to find solitude in the D'Arcy Island or Isle-de-Lis marine parks than elsewhere on a summer weekend, and the sparser use has more to do with the lack of facilities on these islands than with their lack of appeal. Including Portland Island (see the Portland Island chapter) in the route extends the loop 4 miles to the north.

DURATION: Overnight or multiple night.

RATING: Moderate. Currents here can be strong enough to produce tide rips and rough seas when opposing wind from either the north or south.

NAVIGATION AIDS: Canadian Hydrographic Service chart 3310 (small craft strip charts in folio) or 3441 (both 1:40,000); Canadian Hydrographic Service current tables (volume 5) for Race Passage with corrections for Sidney Channel, or Canadian *Current Atlas.*

PLANNING CONSIDERATIONS: Travel with current flows as much as possible (flood goes north). Exploring the lagoon at Sidney Island requires high tide (use Canadian tide table for Fulford Harbour).

Getting There and Launching

Use Tulista Park in Sidney, which is accessible for foot passengers with boats coming from the U.S. on the Washington State ferry. See the Portland Island chapter for details.

Route

Total loop distance is about 18 miles, which can be shortened to 15 miles by eliminating Mandarte amd Rum islands. With an early start and coordination with currents, this loop is feasible for an overnight. A more relaxed itinerary would be allow an additional stop at either Sidney Spit or Isle-de-Lis (Rum Island) marine parks. Water may be available at Sidney Spit, but since the well does run dry in summer, bring enough to last the entire trip.

Sidney Spit makes an interesting (if populated) stop for lunch, or a

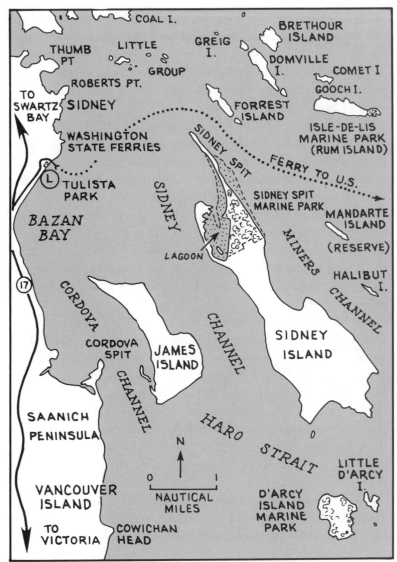

somewhat inconvenient campsite. The campground is located some distance from the water (about 0.2 mile to the nearest sites), and up the hill and south from the dock and picnic area. (The path is smooth enough for boat carts above and below the stairs.) The spit makes interesting exploration on foot at low tide or by paddle. The large lagoon to the south (contained within the park except for a private dock on the north shore and some buildings at the base of the surrounding spit) makes great high-tide paddling, with small channels to explore along the south side. If you are en route to D'Arcy Island from Sidney Spit, consider paddling down the lagoon if the tide is right and then portaging across the spit at the southwest end (about 75 yards, but too rough for boat carts because of old logs).

The remainder of Sidney Island is largely undeveloped, though privately owned. At this writing, only an occasional home is visible along its attractive shorelines or on the bluffs above.

D'Arcy Island Marine Park has no facilities, and is much more lightly visited than either Sidney Spit or Princess Margaret parks to the north. Its south and east sides are the most appealing, with a number of gravel beaches fronting woods and meadows. There are about a half-dozen areas that are suitable for camping. Remains of buildings are found on the brushier west side; a leper colony operated here until the mid-1920s. Due to the chronic fire hazard on this dry island, rely on camp stoves.

A return route via the north side of Sidney Island takes you toward an island that is conspicuously different from all the other islands around it. Mottled chalky sides and a few snags along its crest give slender Mandarte Island the appearance of a derelict dreadnaught. In fact, this steep and rocky island is home to countless nesting birds, including gulls, pigeon guillemots, and rhinoceros auklets. Their droppings give the island its whitewashed appearance and stunt tree growth there. Landings are not allowed on this reserve. Small buildings on the north side and blinds along the crest are used by ornithology researchers.

About 2 miles farther north from Mandarte Island is Isle-de-Lis Marine Park. It is located on Rum Island, which is actually joined to Gooch Island by a short gravel spit. This steep, rocky island has no facilities, but does have suitable tent sites along the south side. There are marginally useful landing sites along that steep and rocky shore, but these will be made precarious by southerly winds, especially at higher tides. You might do better to land on the leeward side of the spit and follow the up-and-down trails over the island.

Near Hood Head

Olympic
Peninsula

Indian Island

Bands of seals, Navy ships, weird nodules in sandstone formations, a fast sluice through a 4-foot-high culvert: all this and more are found along Indian Island's shores. This naval base won a conservation award for management of its wildlands, but look, don't touch: landings are not allowed. No matter—there are a lot of fine opportunities to land elsewhere along this route.

DURATION: Part day or full day.

RATING: Moderate or Protected. Moderate route involves some fastwater paddling and possible tide rips for a short distance.

NAVIGATION AIDS: NOAA charts 18423 SC (1:80,000), 18471 (1:40,000), or 18464 (1:20,000), Port Townsend tide table and Deception Pass current table with corrections for Port Townsend Canal.

PLANNING CONSIDERATIONS: Coordinating your launch time with high tide will dramatically reduce the carrying distance at the Marrowstone Island-Indian Island causeway and will aid in catching favorable currents. At low tide the portage is at least 300 yards of tide flats; high tide reduces it to as little as 50 feet.

Getting There and Launching

Drive to Chimacum, turn east, and drive to Hadlock. Turn right at the stop sign in Hadlock, and then bear left after 0.8 mile to Indian Island.

To launch from Indian Island County Park drive approximately 0.75 mile beyond the Indian Island bridge. Ample parking is available there, with launching on sand or gravel beaches, which are dry for a considerable distance at low tide. (This is also a popular clamming spot.)

To launch near the Marrowstone Island-Indian Island causeway use the county park waysides near there, probably the most suitable start for the Indian Island circumnavigation if the launch is at high tide (see Planning Considerations above). There are a series of wayside turnoffs and paths to the beach on Oak Bay to the south between Indian Island County Park and the causeway. The one about 0.2 mile before the causeway has off-highway parking and a short path giving access to the

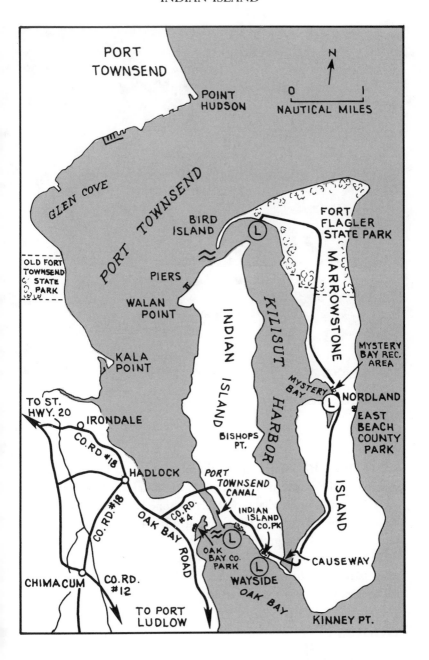

Indian Island's sandstone nodules

Kilisut Harbor tide flats. This is the best site for a high-tide launch starting to the north, or for access to the beach on Oak Bay.

To launch from Nordland on Marrowstone Island, use the Mystery Bay Recreation Area. This state park area has ample parking and easy access to a sand and gravel beach.

To launch from Fort Flagler State Park at the north end of Marrowstone Island, use the boat launch area on Kilisut Harbor. There is parking and easy access to sand and gravel beaches, and to a ramp.

Routes

Indian Island Circumnavigation: *Moderate.* The total paddling distance is 11 miles. Time your trip for high tide at the causeway, whether you start there or not. An effective plan for this trip is to launch at the wayside west of the causeway just after high tide and then head north into Kilisut Harbor. Starting off to the north gets you across the extensive tide flats of the harbor at high water. (The Oak Bay beach is not nearly such a long carry at lower water when you return.) Time your progress paddling north so as to catch the ebb current out of Kilisut Harbor at Fort Flagler State Park. Aim for either the slack or the beginning of the south-flowing flood current in the Port Townsend Canal.

If you catch the tide level at the causeway just right, you can ride the current through one of the two four-foot-wide culverts under the highway. Be careful! The current through here is fast. Be sure that you will have enough headroom and enough water to avoid hanging up on the rocks at either end. But if you opt for discretion instead of this little thrill, the carry over the highway is easy.

Indian Island is an interesting blend of attractive "forbidden fruit" (restricted government property) surrounded by accessible public lands. Most of the island is occupied by the Naval Undersea Warfare Engineering Station, which stores ships' ammunition (reportedly non-nuclear). There are piers and buildings along the northwestern shore, but the remainder of the shoreline is remarkably pristine. The Navy employs a wildlife biologist to manage the island's habitat, and the station won national honors in a Department of Defense conservation award for its management.

However, *landings within the station boundaries are strictly prohibited.* Nonetheless, cruising along the station's shorelines is a pleasant interlude with a largely undisturbed environment, and there are plenty of places on non-Navy property to stretch your legs. Look for river otter along the rocky shores.

The southern end of Indian Island, on both sides, has interesting sandstone formations with embedded nodules of harder rock that have eroded into studded surfaces, some forming tiny bridges like handles. Look for these south of Bishops Point on the Kilisut Harbor side and just north of the Port Townsend Canal on the west side.

Mystery Bay Recreation Area on Marrowstone Island is the first chance for a shore stop, about 2 miles north of the causeway. There are toilets and picnic facilities, and a nearby store at Nordland.

Following the west shore of Indian Island south from Kilisut Harbor involves an hour or so of paddling along shores with no opportunities to get out, so plan for breaks at Fort Flagler beforehand. Fort Flagler has picnic facilities, bathrooms with running water, and a concession stand that sells snacks during the summer months. The western edge of the harbor is a low sand spit covered with grass and connected to the park at low tide. Called Bird Island locally, it has a popular place for large groups of seals to haul out at its southern end. Paddling out through the channel, you may find yourself surrounded by 50 or more of them.

Be sure to honor the Navy's requirement that you stay 600 feet from their docks at Walan Point. The next complex of docks, at Crane Point about 1 mile south, has no such distance restriction. Just beyond is an inviting park facility, but it's for naval personnel only.

You could make a 1.5-mile detour west to Hadlock before entering Port Townsend Canal. There is a private marina, a very popular shoreside cafe, and the town itself a few blocks up from the water.

The Navy's property line on Indian Island turns inland at the midpoint of a shell beach just north of the narrows of Port Townsend Canal. Just south are excellent stops ashore in the beginning of the county's parklands here. Also south of the beach is the old Indian-Marrowstone ferry landing.

Port Townsend Canal has currents of up to 3 knots. There are shore eddies except between the jetties at the southern end, where you will have no choice but to fight the current if it is against you, unless the water level is high enough to paddle behind the jetty on the Indian Island side. Fairly large rips (standing waves) can form in the channel at the downstream end of the narrows, which may be dangerous to kayakers not experienced with rough water.

Adjoining the southern end of the canal are Oak Bay County Park on the west side and Indian Island County Park on the east side. These have outhouses and picnic tables, and the sand and gravel tide flats are productive clamming areas.

Fort Flagler State Park Local Paddling: *Protected.* Choose your own paddling distance. This area is popular for short trips in the warmer protected waters, and a good place for new paddlers to work on their skills. Be careful of the entrance channel to Kilisut Harbor, which can run at more than 1 knot.

Hood Head

An interesting lagoon and a gravel spit (both preserved in an undeveloped state park), plus easy access make this a nice afternoon's destination for western Puget Sound residents. Ducks, herons, and other waterfowl are plentiful in the lagoon during the winter months. The alongshore paddling and largely protected waters make this a suitable trip for new kayakers. It could be combined with others in the area, such as the Salisbury Point-Port Gamble or Port Ludlow-Mats Mats Bay trips (see the Port Gamble and Mats Mats Bay chapters).

DURATION: Part day.
RATING: Protected.
NAVIGATION AIDS: NOAA chart 18477 (1:25,000) or 18445 SC (1:80,000); Port Townsend tide table.
PLANNING CONSIDERATIONS: Midtide or higher required to explore the lagoon.

Launching a kite en route to Hood Head

Getting There and Launching

Access is simple: just turn down Termination Point Road immediately north of the west end of the Hood Canal Bridge. Follow it north past a Puget Power substation to Shine Public Tidelands. Managed by the Washington State Parks and Recreation Commission, this area has parking, pit toilets, and 20 RV-style campsites along the shore. Launch on the gravel beach.

Routes

Lagoon Round Trip: *Protected*. Paddling distance is 4 miles. Follow the beach north to the entrance just short of the spit connecting Hood Head to the mainland. You may encounter some current at the entrance to the lagoon, but probably not enough to cause any problems. At higher tides you can paddle southwest to grassy flats bordering alder forest that make a good spot for a picnic stop, some bird-watching, and exploration ashore in this undeveloped state park. An abandoned house is concealed in the brush on the west side of the lagoon.

Hood Head Circumnavigation: *Protected*. Add 2 miles to the lagoon round trip. Rounding Hood Head, perhaps on your way back to the launch point, will give you some different perspectives on Hood Canal—a fine view north toward Marrowstone Island and south along the canal past Bangor. And you might get as close as you ever will to a passing Trident submarine, certain to be an awesome and intimidating sight from your little craft. You will be able to paddle across the spit only on the highest tides; otherwise a short carry is needed above mid-tide. Mud flats are extensive south of the spit on the lowest tides. Some of the tidelands south of Point Hannon are privately owned and are so marked.

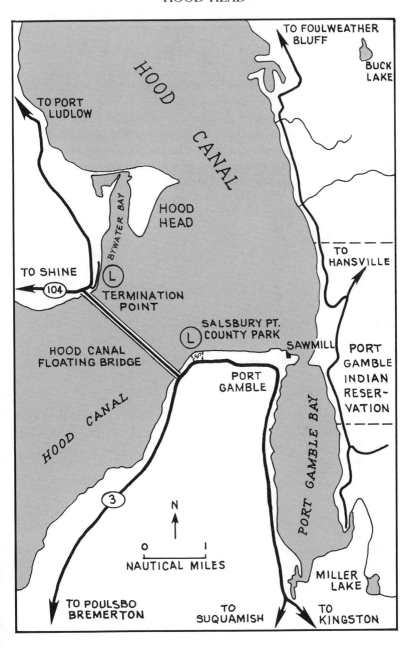

Port Gamble

Port Gamble, at the mouth of Hood Canal, has the oldest operating sawmill in North America, established in 1853. At the turn of the century, this bay was busy with lumber schooners like Seattle's *Wawona* being loaded for destinations up and down the Pacific Coast. Paddling by this still-busy mill, you can see the historic Victorian buildings in the background while you watch logs climb the chain on their way from the log pond to the saws. This route could be combined with Hood Head (see the Hood Head chapter), using launch sites on either side of Hood Canal (the crossing would rate a Moderate).

DURATION: Part day.
RATING: Protected.
NAVIGATION AIDS: NOAA charts 18445 SC, 18441 (both 1:80,000), or 18477 (1:25,000); Seattle tide table (subtract five minutes).
PLANNING CONSIDERATIONS: Go anytime.

Getting There and Launching

Use Salsbury Point County Park, located 0.5 mile north of the Hood Canal Bridge. Launch either at the ramp (the more difficult choice if there is a shore break) or the sand beach in the south end of the park (requires a 100-yard carry across the lawn).

Route

One-way distance to the entrance to Port Gamble Bay is about 1.5 miles. Paddle as far as desired into the bay. Note that there are no public tidelands or shores on this route once you leave the county park. The entrance to the bay narrows to scarcely more than 100 yards, with the mill's docks on the south and a gravel spit to the north. The spit and lands north and south of it are part of the Port Gamble Indian Reservation, and are not open to access without permission. The north shore of Port Gamble Bay is mostly residential and farmland. The south side is largely undeveloped and wooded, with barge hulks and occasional

Sawmill, Port Gamble

beaches. Just south of the sawmill's log storage area is a section of the Hood Canal floating bridge. Others were kept here while the bridge was undergoing rebuilding following its destruction in the winter of 1979–1980.

Mats Mats Bay

This quiet little bay north of Port Ludlow is just right for paddling practice or touring anchored yachts. The mood is pastoral, with residences generally low-key and set back from the shore. A narrow, tree-lined entrance leads out to interesting offshore rocks (less than 0.5 mile away) that are popular with divers. This local trip could be extended by paddling to or from Port Ludlow, about 3 miles away, perhaps with a car shuttle return.

DURATION: Part day.
RATING: Protected.
NAVIGATION AIDS: NOAA chart 18445 SC (1:80,000, see 1:40,000 inset).
PLANNING CONSIDERATIONS: Go anytime.

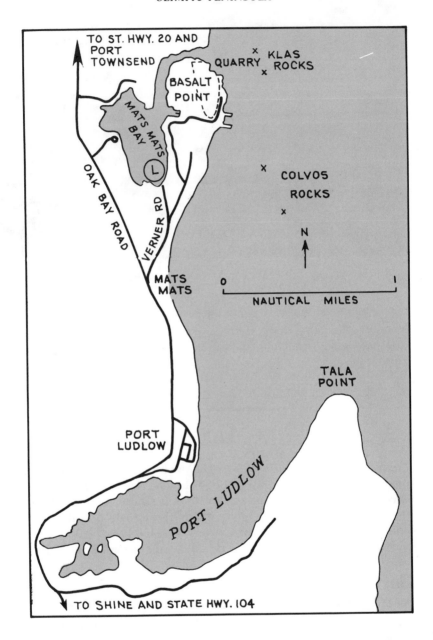

Getting There and Launching

From Highway 104, turn north on Paradise Bay Road just west of the Hood Canal Bridge. Follow this 6 miles, passing Port Ludlow, to the intersection with Oak Bay Road. Turn right and go another 2 miles and turn right on Verner Road. Go 0.5 mile to the launching ramp in Mats Mats Bay.

Route

Suit your fancy here. The bay and entrance are plenty to see on their own, making a 2-mile loop if you follow the shore. Or paddle out to Klas and Colvos rocks if the weather isn't windy (these are nicest to explore on calm days), or south toward Port Ludlow. Colvos Rock, the largest of the offshore rocks in the area, is itself a poor place to get out of your boat—it's about 50 feet across, barren, and too steep for easy landings. The round trip to Colvos Rock from the Mats Mats Bay boat launch is 3 miles.

Boat launch, Mats Mats Bay

The entrance to the bay narrows to less than 100 yards with range markers to guide larger craft through. There are a few homes on the northern shore, and the naturalness of the south side is marred by the scars of a quarry that can be seen through the trees.

This quarry and gravel operation occupies the real estate for almost a mile south of the bay entrance. Though there are a few beaches here that are unaffected by the work behind, do not go ashore.

Central Hood Canal
QUILCENE AND DABOB BAYS, DOSEWALLIPS, PLEASANT HARBOR, AND SCENIC BEACH

With the Olympic Range towering overhead, this part of Hood Canal is the epitome of the meeting place for land and sea. When you can take your eyes off this gorgeous backdrop, there is lots to look at up close: rich estuaries, lagoons, and a tideland that is renowned for its oysters. Be careful where you collect them; most tidelands in Hood Canal are private. Oysters are usually open to harvesting (shuck and leave the shells where taken) from mid-September to mid-July. Check current Department of Fisheries regulations for the current season and local exceptions in this area.

DURATION: Part day to full day.
RATING: Protected or Moderate. Moderate route involves crossing 1.5 to 3 miles of open water.
NAVIGATION AIDS: NOAA charts 18476 (1:40,000) or 18445 SC (1:80,000); Seattle tide table (add five to 15 minutes).
PLANNING CONSIDERATIONS: Best at high tide.

Getting There and Launching

Launch from either the east or west shore of Hood Canal, depending on which is most convenient.

On the west side, at least four alternatives are off Highway 101 between Quilcene and Pleasant Harbor. For exploring upper Quilcene Bay, launch at Quilcene Haven boat ramp. Take Rogers Road, then go

Pleasant Harbor

left on Linger Longer Road. Follow it 1.5 miles to this small boat harbor.

Use Point Whitney for access to Dabob Bay or for paddling south toward Dosewallips or Pleasant Harbor. From Quilcene, follow Highway 101 south 8 miles to Bee Mill Road (marked for Point Whitney). Turn left and go 2.5 miles to the Washington Department of Fisheries Shellfish Lab at Point Whitney. The gravel beach here is fine for launching in all but strong northerly winds, when shore break may be quite large. Public rest rooms are nearby.

Though there are roads to the shores of upper Dabob Bay, launching there to paddle this interesting area is not advised, since both the tidelands and shores are private and local owners are concerned about trespassing on the rich oyster beds.

At Dosewallips State Park, launch in the high-tide channels adjacent to the day-use area. In Pleasant Harbor, use the dock at Pleasant Harbor State Park. This otherwise-undeveloped park is not marked from Highway 101; to get there turn off Highway 101 onto a narrow lane

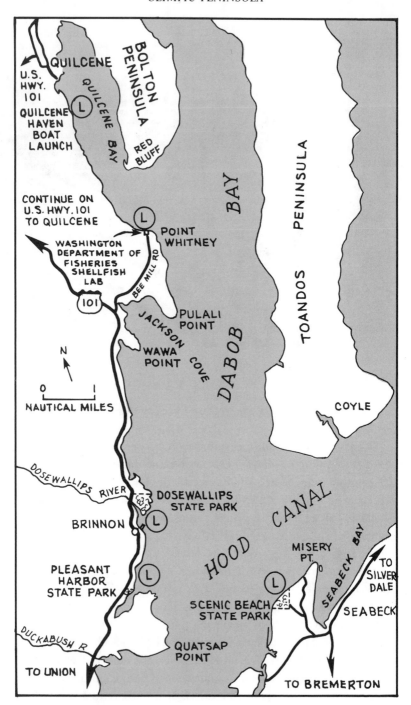

about 2 miles south of Dosewallips State Park—next to a white building signed "Pleasant Harbor View"—and descend carefully to the small unpaved parking lot.

On the east shore, use Scenic Beach State Park near Seabeck. From Highway 3 in Silverdale, take the Trigger Avenue exit. Go right 0.5 mile and turn left on Old Frontier Road. Go almost 2 miles to Anderson Hill Road, and turn right. Follow this 4 miles to its end, and turn right on Seabeck Highway. Another 3 miles brings you to the small center of Seabeck, which has the closest store for the launch point. Go another 0.5 mile and turn right on Scenic Beach Road. Finally, drive another 1.5 miles to the park. Continue straight past the park entrance to the last lot. Carry boats through the picnic area about 150 yards to steps leading to a small gravel beach. Water and rest rooms are provided here.

Routes

Scenic Beach–Dosewallips–Pleasant Harbor Triangle: *Moderate.* Distance is 8 miles. Start at any of these three points of the triangle. Both Scenic Beach and Pleasant Harbor are fine at any stage of the tide, but access to the water at Dosewallips is feasible only at high tide and stops there are much more pleasant when the extensive tidal flats of this estuary are covered. All three make pleasant lunch stops. Scenic Beach State Park has the most extensive and convenient facilities.

Those at Dosewallips are a short walk from the water if you are able to paddle up the river about 0.25 mile or up one of the dead-end side channels to the south of the river at high tide. The river channel enters Hood Canal in the southern portion of the estuary, and the park's day-use facilities are located on the south side of the river. The portion of the estuary north of the river channel is primarily private land.

Tiny Pleasant Harbor is worth a little time to explore its back reaches and to look over the variety of yachts and workboats that use this all-weather shelter. The park is just inside and west of the narrow entrance, and consists primarily of the dock and a dusty parking lot above it (with outhouse).

Quilcene to Dosewallips: *Protected.* Distance is 5 miles. Start from Point Wilson, perhaps with a short side trip into the narrow lagoon entered from the end of the beach just west of the laboratory buildings. The rocky and largely undeveloped shores south of the lab to Pulali Point are some of the more interesting ones in the area. Keep going around the flats of the Dosewallips estuary to the south side before going ashore to avoid the private lands there.

Quilcene to Dabob Bay: *Protected*. Round-trip distance is from 3 to 10 miles, depending on how deeply into northern Dabob Bay you care to explore. The only place you can go ashore is the public tidelands at the southeast end of the Bolton Peninsula, east of Red Bluffs. This 0.5-mile state tideland is best identified by the lack of private tidelands signs that define its limits. The shores above are private. All other tidelands in Dabob Bay are private, so remember that you will be trespassing anywhere that you touch bottom.

Southern Hood Canal

ANNAS BAY

Annas Bay, the elbow of the Great Bend of Hood Canal, has the largest river estuary (the Skokomish River) in the area. Set against the spectacular backdrop of the incredibly nearby Olympics, this maze of winding channels and grassy banks abounds in bird life and seals, and the fall colors of the wetland deciduous trees and shrubs make a brilliant contrast against the mountains' greens. At high tide, a meandering route can be followed all the way across the estuary through these channels and islets.

DURATION: Part day.
RATING: Protected.
NAVIGATION AIDS: NOAA charts 18476 (1:40,000) or 18445 SC (1:80,000); Seattle tide table (add 10 minutes).
PLANNING CONSIDERATIONS: Best at high tide.

Getting There and Launching

Launch from sites in or near the town of Union along Highway 106 or at Potlatch State Park on Highway 101. Car-shuttle distance between these areas is about 5 miles. In Union, use the public boat ramp

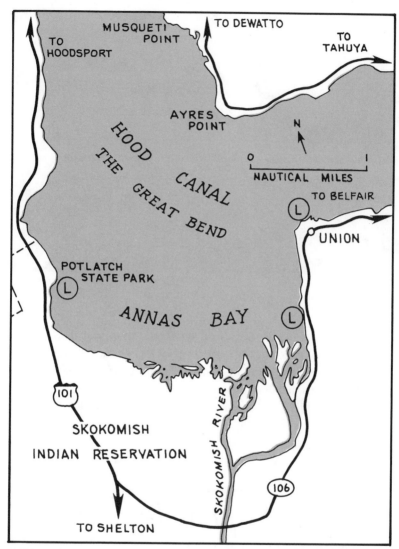

and lot. An informal roadside pullout along Highway 106 about 1 mile south of Union gives the closest access to the eastern end of the estuary. In Potlatch State Park, use the beach in the day-use area.

Route

One-way paddling distance across the estuary is about 2.5 miles. Add another mile if you start from Union. The tidelands in the estuary are

Annas Bay

the property of the Skokomish Indian Reservation, and there may be many gill nets set across the river channels during the fall salmon runs. Depending on the tide height, pick your route along the fringe of channels and islands defining the northern edge of the estuary. If the water level is fairly high, you should be able to make it all the way across within these, except at the center where a causeway requires you to skirt to the outside open water.

Sequim Bay

This quiet bay has the backdrop of the Olympics to the south and Protection Island and distant Dungeness Spit to the north. A huge lagoon almost landlocked by two sand spits at its entrance, Sequim Bay provides unlimited opportunities for exploring its wooded and residential shorelines or the sand spits. These and an associated tidal lagoon allow plenty of shallow-water paddling and stops ashore at two public beaches. Using a shuttle (road distance is 5 miles), a 3-mile paddle along bluffs to the bay's entrance can be made, beginning at Marlyn

Nelson Park north of Sequim Bay and ending at John Wayne Marina inside of it. This could be extended another 2 miles by ending at Sequim Bay State Park deeper inside the bay.

DURATION: Part day.
RATING: Protected. Confined waters and alongshore routes make this a good place for new kayakers looking for an easy scenic paddle with few likely challenges.
NAVIGATION AIDS: NOAA chart 18465 (1:80,000) or 18471 (1:40,000); Port Townsend tide table (subtract 30 minutes).
PLANNING CONSIDERATIONS: A rising tide is best for exploring the lagoon behind Gibson Spit. Launch from John Wayne Marina and stay within the bay and lagoon if seas to the north of Travis Spit are rough.

Travis Spit, looking west toward Gibson Spit

Getting There and Launching

John Wayne Marina, Sequim Bay State Park, and Marlyn Nelson Park are launch alternatives for this route.

The marina, on land donated to the county by the actor, is off Highway 101 about 2 miles east of Sequim. The turn from the highway is well marked; then follow signs about 1 mile to the marina. Use the ramp for launching.

Sequim Bay State Park lies on both sides of Highway 101 about 4 miles east of Sequim. Turn east off the highway (toward the water) and follow the road downhill through the campground to the boat launch, or turn right to the picnic area and launch on the beach.

Marlyn Nelson Park is reached by turning north from Highway 101 onto Brown Road about 0.5 mile east of Sequim. Follow it 1 mile to Port Williams Road, turn right, and go about 2.5 miles to the park. Launch from the gravel beach.

Route

Beginning at either Sequim Bay State Park or John Wayne Marina, paddle north along the beach. Shores between these points and the bay's entrance are wooded, with occasional homes above the gravel beaches. About 1 mile north of the marina are Battelle Institute's laboratories, located just inside the dredged entrance that skirts the end of Travis Spit (Kiapot Point), a long sand and gravel obstruction that extends from the east shore nearly to the bay's western side. Just north is a smaller one—Gibson Spit—running perpendicular to Travis Spit from the north and further constricting the entrance. At the Battelle labs, you could either cut across to explore the north side of the spit or continue along the shore to the lagoon and Gibson Spit. This is a narrow dredged channel, so stay close to shore to assure that larger boats will have the room they need.

The two spits have public tidelands: on the north side of Travis Spit and the east side of Gibson Spit. The areas of both above the mean high-tide line are the property of Battelle Institute, which does research there from time to time, and they ask that you not trespass on them.

The lagoon is a fine place to ride in on a rising tide (start in at midtide), with good bird viewing and a pastoral backdrop of farmlands. At

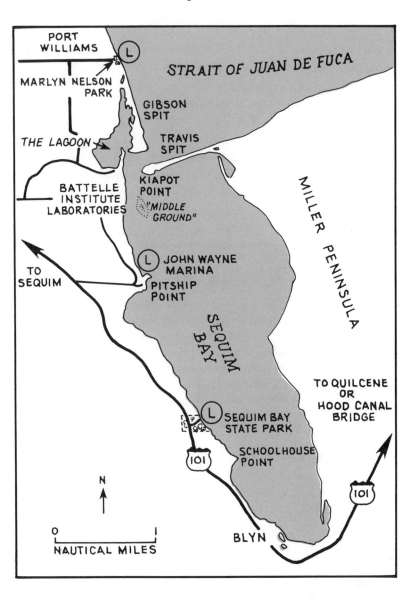

high tide you should be able to follow the tidal channels for a mile or so. The tidelands in the lagoon west of Gibson Spit are also research areas, as is the drying shoal called Middle Ground south of Travis Spit. Stay in your boat except on the public tidelands. Though shellfish are plentiful in Sequim Bay, they cannot be harvested because of contamination.

The route from Gibson Spit to Marlyn Nelson Park follows the gravel beach north. Bluffs begin at the foot of the spit, less than 1 mile south of the park. The park's present site was once Port Williams, where steamers called with freight and passenger service for the community of Sequim.

There are other route alternatives in Sequim Bay. For instance, you could make an upper bay loop from either the marina or Sequim Bay Park, paddling across the bay (crossing about 1.5 miles of open water) to the largely residential east shore and then following the shore around the south end, or cutting back across at some point.

Dungeness Spit

This 5-mile-long spit is a national wildlife refuge set aside for waterfowl and shorebirds. As many as 10,000 winter in the refuge, particularly the black brant. Sandpipers and other shorebirds scour its beaches for food. Shallow Dungeness Bay, south of the spit, harbors clams, oysters, and the crab that takes its name. Paddling the full length of the spit makes a fine day trip, with a stop for lunch at the New Dungeness lighthouse near the end.

DURATION: Part day or full day. No camping is allowed along these shorelines.

RATING: Protected to Moderate, depending on route. Moderate route may involve exposure to rough seas, beach surf, and tide rips.

NAVIGATION AIDS: NOAA chart 18471 (1:40,000); Port Townsend tide tables (subtract about 45 minutes).

PLANNING CONSIDERATIONS: Best on higher tides. Tide flats south of the spit and in the lagoon are extensive at low tide.

Getting There and Launching

From Highway 101 in Sequim, turn south on Sequim Avenue and go 6 miles. This becomes Sequim-Dungeness Way and later Marine Drive. After 6 miles, the spit comes into view on the right. Turn down a side

Dungeness Bay, with Dungeness Spit in the background

road that drops sharply over the bluff to Cline Spit County Park and launch from the gravel beach north of the parking area.

If you plan to go ashore in the refuge, you must purchase a permit (or use a Golden Eagle or Golden Age pass or a federal duck stamp if you have one). Daily permits are available at the trailhead to the base of the spit in Dungeness Recreation Area, a Clallam County park. To get there, continue on Marine Drive, which then turns left, becoming Old Town Road. Turn right on the Dungeness Scenic Loop and follow it to the park entrance. There is also a campground here, though too distant from the water for paddle-in use.

Route

In windy weather, you may prefer to stick to the lagoon north and east of Cline Spit, which affords sheltered paddling yet easy access to the

On the beach at the end of Dungeness Spit

beaches north and south of the spit. The south side of the spit usually is calm except in southerly winds. The manned lighthouse at the end of the spit is open to the public on weekends and holidays. The climb up the tower's spiral staircase is worthwhile in its own right; the view along the spit is even better.

In calm weather, consider a circumnavigation of the spit (about 6 miles by the route described). Because most of the spit is narrow, a portage across can cut the trip as short as you like. The feasibility of this depends on the surf on the northern beach. Paddle due north from Cline Spit and walk across to check the condition of the surf to the north, which may well be big enough to get you wet when going through it even if you are experienced with surf. If it seems too big, paddle east along the inside of the spit to the lagoon's eastern reaches (tide height allowing) and portage to the south side of the spit.

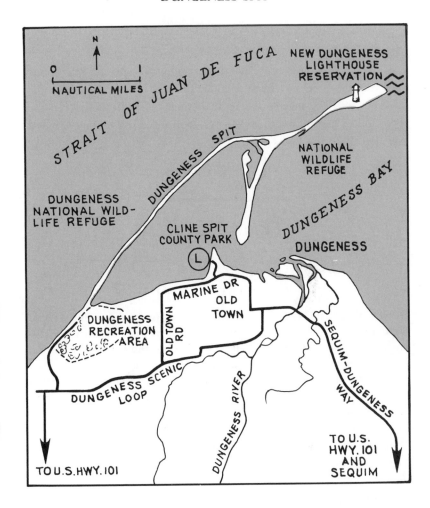

Paddling the northern side of Dungeness Spit allows a close-up look at this wild, driftwood-strewn beach, staying as close in as the surf allows. Keep an eye offshore for wakes from the constant stream of ships passing in and out of the Strait of Juan de Fuca, as these will break farther out. With an eye to seaward, you can play "chicken" with the surf, gauging your distance from the beach to position yourself just beyond where the waves break. The rapid rise and fall of a steepening wave is exhilarating, and the feel of the wave as it breaks beneath your shoreward paddle blade is a little thrill. Be ready to cut to seaward for bigger waves, or else you will be washed onto the beach and probably drenched.

Currents passing over the bar at the end of the spit and interacting with the eddies behind it can produce bad tide rips there on both the flood and ebb. You may be able to avoid them by cutting across close to shore unless seas are rough. Better yet, look ahead and portage across if you don't like the looks of it.

Crescent Bay to Freshwater Bay
(STRIPED PEAK AREA)

Here is a taste of Washington's outer coast, just a few miles west of Port Angeles. Swells penetrating the Strait of Juan de Fuca are still large enough here to make challenging surf on the area's beaches and pack enough power to bore a double sea arch along this route. Depending on the swell size, landings are possible on many tiny gravel beaches along the way that are inaccessible from the cliffs above. Preservation of the uplands as the Department of Natural Resources' Striped Peak Recreation Area makes this one of the wildest stretches along the Strait of Juan de Fuca coast.

DURATION: Part day (add time for car shuttle or double the route distance for a paddled return).

RATING: Exposed. Surf and strong currents are likely. Surf may prevent landings along the route and commit you to paddling in the current, exposed to the effects of wind (and problems of opposing current) for the full distance between Crescent and Freshwater bays.

NAVIGATION AIDS: NOAA chart 18465 (1:80,000); Race Rocks current table (adjusted for Angeles Point) or the Canadian *Current Atlas.*

PLANNING CONSIDERATIONS: Travel with the current direction or at times of little current, as forecasted in the current tables or the *Current Atlas.* Alongshore currents can exceed 2 knots, and breaking

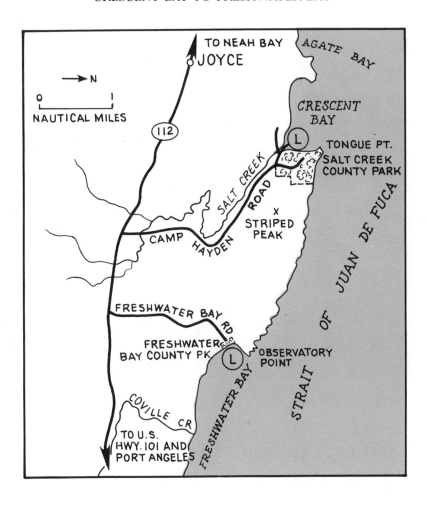

swells may prevent using inshore eddies to work upstream. A large swell (swell size is usually included in marine forecasts for the Pacific Coast) may produce large and unavoidable surf at Crescent Bay and may prevent landings along the way. Avoid weather conditions when strong east or west winds are forecast for the Strait of Juan de Fuca.

Crescent Bay from Tongue Point

Getting There and Launching

This route can be accessed from either Freshwater Bay to the east or Crescent Bay to the west. Neither launch point allows overnight parking (camping is provided at Salt Creek County Park at Crescent Bay). An easy 9-mile vehicle shuttle could be made between them. To get to the area, take Highway 112 west from its junction with Highway 101 a few miles west of Port Angeles. After 5 miles, turn right on Freshwater Bay Road and follow it 3 miles to Freshwater Bay County Park. Launching is on a gravel beach next to the launching ramp.

For Crescent Bay, continue another 3 miles on Highway 112 to Camp Hayden Road. Turn right and go 3 miles to Salt Creek County Park. Continue straight for the park or turn left for the launching point. The park provides a large number of campsites (many of which are sited spectacularly at the edge of sea cliffs with panoramic views of the strait) and access to extensive tide pools at Tongue Point. This area has unique coast defense artillery installations that are well worth a visit. These were built during World War II rather than prior to the First World War as in the case of others farther inland.

The best launch point in Crescent Bay is from a small parking lot next to Salt Creek. At low tide, it is necessary to follow the creek (often too low to float a kayak) about 300 yards down the beach to the water. Surf here can be significant, depending on swell size and weather, though refraction behind the rocks near tongue point may give some protection at midtide.

If conditions appear too daunting at Crescent Bay, a shorter trip out of Freshwater Bay is probably wiser and certainly less effort. Protected from the west, Freshwater Bay usually offers calm launching and a chance to visit as much of the wild coast to the west as is comfortable (swells and shore break generally increase to the west toward Crescent Bay).

The coast between Crescent and Freshwater bays

Route

The Exposed rating is merited by the swells, which can make landings along this 4-mile route difficult and could commit you to reaching one end or the other if the weather takes a turn for the worst, and by the current.

Planning with the current is more important here than along other routes where it is possible to use eddies to travel against contrary flows. Extensive kelp beds border this entire coastline. Unless the swells are very small, surge and shore break prevent using the eddies inside the kelp, committing you to traveling along the outside of the beds where the current is strong.

Cliffs with tiny gravel pocket beaches here and there are continuous between Observatory Point at Freshwater Bay and Tongue Point at Crescent Bay. The most interesting landing spots are at the midpoint of the route, near a double arch best reached from a beach just to the east.

Be especially watchful for intermittent breakers on offshore rocks while rounding Tongue Point. Since swells vary in size, these rocks may allow smaller ones to pass without breaking, making them unnoticeable until a big one arrives. Note their position on the chart, try to spot them when they do break, and give them a wide berth.

Appendices

CALCULATING CURRENTS USING NOAA'S TABLES

The example shown is for June 3, 1985, a day of particularly strong currents, at San Juan Island's Limestone Point (see Stuart Island chapter). In the lower portion of the table, corrections for Limestone Point (Spieden Channel) are based on daily predictions for San Juan Channel (the upper portion of the table). One hour is added to the calculations for daylight saving time. To calculate the first slack for Limestone Point, take the slack water time for San Juan Channel (A), minus the correction time for the minimum current before the ebb at Limestone

SAN JUAN CHANNEL (south entrance), WASHINGTON, 1985

F-Flood, Dir. 010° True   E-Ebb, Dir. 180° True

JUNE

Day	Slack Water Time	Maximum Current Time Vel.	
	h.m.	h.m.	knots
1 Sa	0214 0922 1630 2210	0555 1237 1910	4.2E 4.6F 2.5E
2 Su	0250 1004 1726 2309	0024 0639 1325 2004	2.0F 4.3E 4.9F 2.5E
3 M	0328 **A** 1047 **G** 1819	0113 0724 **C** 1415 2057	1.6F 4.3E **E** 5.0F **I** 2.5E

CURRENT DIFFERENCES AND OTHER CONSTANTS, 1985

NO.	PLACE	TIME DIFFERENCES				SPEED RATIOS	
		Min. before Flood	Flood	Min. before Ebb	Ebb	Flood	Ebb
		h. m.	h. m.	h. m.	h. m.		
	SAN JUAN CHANNEL	on SAN JUAN CHANNEL, p.58					
1655	Cattle Point, 1.2 miles southeast of....	+0 11	-0 20	+0 34	-0 01	0.3	0.9
1660	SAN JUAN CHANNEL (south entrance).......	Daily Predictions					
1665	Kings Point, Lopez Island, 1 mile NNW of	+0 51	-0 07	+0 27	+0 36	0.6	0.5
1670	Pear Point, 1.1 miles east of...........	+0 40	+1 09	-0 10	+1 01	0.4	0.5
1675	Turn Rock Light, 1.9 miles northwest of.	+1 19	+1 22	+0 20	-0 01	0.4	0.5
1680	Crane Island, south of, Wasp Passage....	-0 10	+0 35	+0 29	+0 07	0.2	0.1
1685	Wasp Passage Light, 0.5 mile WSW of.....	+0 19	+0 28	+0 15	-0 15	0.5	0.4
1690	Spring Passage, south entrance..........	+0 04	-1 09	-0 43	-0 13	0.4	0.4
1695	Limestone Point, Spieden Channel........	+0 23**H**	-0 12	-1 00 **B**	+0 26 **D**	0.7**J**	1.2**F**

Point (B), plus one hour for daylight saving time (DST).

$$0328 - 1\ 00\ (1\ \text{hour}\ 0\ \text{minutes}) + 1\ 00\ (\text{DST}) = 0328.$$

To calculate the maximum ebb current for Limestone Point, take the maximum current time for San Juan Channel (C), plus the maximum ebb current correction for Limestone Point (D), plus one hour for daylight saving time (DST).

$$0724 + 0\ 26\ (\text{minutes}) + 1\ 00\ (\text{DST}) = 0850.$$

To calculate the speed in knots for that time, take the maximum current velocity for San Juan Channel (E), multiplied by the ebb speed ratio for Limestone Point (F).

$$4.3 \times 1.2 = 5.2.$$

To calculate when the next slack for Limestone Point will occur, take the next slack water time for San Juan Channel (G), minus the correction time for the minimum current before the flood for Limestone Point (H), plus one hour for daylight saving time (DST).

$$1047 + 0\ 23\ (\text{minutes}) + 1\ 00\ (\text{DST}) = 1210.$$

Note that the interval of this large exchange is almost nine hours. Though the afternoon flood current will be 5 knots in San Juan Channel, Spieden Channel will be slower than during the morning ebb. To calculate the speed in knots for that time, take the maximum current velocity for San Juan Channel (I), multiplied by the flood speed ratio for Limestone Point (J).

$$5.0 \times 0.7 = 3.2.$$

USEFUL PUBLICATIONS

Canadian Hydrographic Service. *Current Atlas: Juan de Fuca Strait to Strait of Georgia.* Ottawa: Canadian Hydrographic Service Department of Fisheries and Oceans, 1983.
This atlas provides the most accurate and detailed information on tidal currents in this complex region. For a given hour and tidal range, the user is directed to a chart showing currents at that time. Calculations required to arrive at the correct chart make this resource a bit difficult to use. (See *Washburne's Tables* for a simplified method of finding the proper current chart.)

Chettleburgh, Peter. *An Explorer's Guide: Marine Parks of British Columbia.* Vancouver, B.C.: Maclean Hunter, 1985. Some of the best detail available on the history and attractions of these parks, especially those not covered in other resources listed here.

Cummings, Al, and Bailey-Cummings, Jo. *Gunkholing in the Gulf Islands.* Edmonds, Washington: Nor'westing, 1989 (revised). Done with the same wit and eclectic detail as their San Juans book.

————. *Gunkholing in the San Juans.* Edmonds, Washington: Nor'westing (No date). This boater's guide includes a lot of local lore not found elsewhere. It is written in a friendly and entertaining style.

Department of Natural Resources, State of Washington. Public tideland booklets: *North Puget Sound,* 1978; *San Juan Island Region,* 1985; *South Puget Sound,* 1978; *Strait of Juan de Fuca,* 1984.
These booklets are handy for identifying public tidelands and DNR upland picnic or camping facilities. The tidelands are primarily of interest for shellfish gathering or just a place to stretch your legs at low tide. They are of little use to you when the tide is high because the uplands are usually private. The booklets are available by writing to:
Photos, Maps, and Reports
Capitol Park Building
1063 South Capitol Way AW-11
Olympia, WA 98504
(206) 753-5338

Ince, John, and Kottner, Hedi. *Sea Kayaking Canada's West Coast.* Vancouver, B.C.: Raxas Books, 1982.
  The original sea kayaker's classic guidebook for the coast, with trips liberally scattered up and down the B.C. coast, including the Gulf Islands.

Island Canoe Company. *Current and Tide Tables for Puget Sound, Deception Pass, the San Juans, Gulf Islands, and Strait of Juan de Fuca.* Bainbridge Island, Washington: Island Canoe Company, published annually.
  This collection of local tide and current information is otherwise available only in large NOAA volumes.

————. *The New San Juan Current Guide Including the Gulf Islands and Strait of Juan de Fuca.* Bainbridge Island, Washington: Island Canoe Company, 1985.
  The charts in this publication show currents with correction factors for local slack times and speeds.

————. *Puget Sound Current Guide.* Bainbridge Island, Washington: Island Canoe Company, 1984.
  This publication includes the same information for Puget Sound as found in the above publication.

Lilly, Kenneth E., Jr. *Marine Weather of Western Washington.* Seattle: Starpath School of Navigation, 1983.
  Lilly's book provides some of the most helpful information ever for understanding the patterns and idiosyncrasies of western Washington's weather and learning about how weather features happen. It is essential if you want to go beyond just listening to forecasts for weather prediction, and it also includes useful information on waves.

McGary, Noel, and Lincoln, John W. *Tide Prints: Surface Tidal Currents in Puget Sound.* Seattle: University of Washington Press, 1977 (out of print).
  This book, with its separate charts showing currents at different points in the tide cycle, complements the Canadian Hydrographic Service's *Current Atlas: Juan de Fuca Strait to Strait of Georgia.* Unfortunately, the book is out of print at this writing. Check local libraries for a copy.

Mueller, Marge. *The San Juan Islands Afoot and Afloat.* 2d ed. Seattle: The Mountaineers, 1988.

Mueller, Marge and Ted. *North Puget Sound Afoot and Afloat.* Seattle: The Mountaineers, 1988.

————. *South Puget Sound Afoot and Afloat.* Seattle: The Mountaineers, 1983.
————. *Middle Puget Sound Afoot and Afloat.* Seattle: The Mountaineers, 1990.

These four companion volumes provide comprehensive coverage of each area; just about any place worth mentioning is included. They also include good information about facilities and services on shore.

Obee, Bruce. *The Gulf Islands Explorer.* 4th ed. North Vancouver, B.C.: Whitecap Books, 1988.
A good how-and-where reference for the major islands, with information and ideas for kayaks and canoes.

Saltwater Access Map. Snohomish, Washington: Snohomish Publishing Co., 1984.
Primarily oriented toward launch and marina facilities for fishermen, this map is helpful for spotting put-ins and take-outs. The information on public upland facilities (e.g., camping) is spotty.

Tidelog: Puget Sound Edition. Tiburon, California: Pacific Publishers, published annually.
This is a useful combination of tide and current information for the year. It provides daily tidal curves that show slacks and associated current strengths and lunar and solar phases as they affect tides. It also includes current charts for Puget Sound and current schedules for Deception Pass and the Narrows at Tacoma.

U.S. Department of Commerce, National Oceanic and Atmospheric Administration. *Tidal Current Tables: Pacific Coast of North America and Asia.* Washington, D.C.: Government Printing Office, published annually.
This volume includes current information for local points

throughout the Northwest, as well as the rest of the Pacific coast. See Island Canoe Company publications if you are interested in Washington's inland waters only.

Washburne's Tables. Bellevue, Washington: Weatherly Press, published annually.

Use these tables in conjunction with the helpful Canadian Hydrographic Service's *Current Atlas: Juan de Fuca Strait to Strait of Georgia.* These tables provide direct access to the proper current chart at any hour of any day without need for calculations or adjustment for daylight saving time.

INDEX

INDEX

About the author:

Randy Washburne is a veteran sea kayaker and the author of two other books, *The Coastal Kayaker's Manual* and *The Coastal Kayaker,* as well as *Washburne's Tables,* popular regional current guides, and numerous magazine articles on kayaking. He teaches sea kayaking and navigation and manufactures canoe and kayak accessories in Seattle, Washington.

Call or send for catalog of more than 200 outdoor books published by:
The Mountaineers
1011 S.W. Klickitat Way, Suite 107
Seattle WA 98134
1-800-553-4453